Giving up the Ghost

"LET US CLASP HANDS OVER THE BLOODY CHASM."—HORACE GREELEY.

Political cartoonist, Thomas Nast, waved the bloody shirt of Andersonville in this attack on candidate Horace Greeley in the presidential campaign of 1872.

Andersonville

Giving up the Ghost

Contributing Editors;

William Styple, Nancy Styple, Jack Fitzpatrick, Bill Dekker,
Mike Bub, Bruce Jones, Gerry Mason, Peter Doroshenko,
Bill Mapes, Jim Nevins, John Kuhl, Rob Hodge, Larry Sangi

Belle Grove Publishing Co.
Kearny, N.J.
1996

© 1996 Belle Grove Publishing Company
All rights reserved
Printed in the United States of America
Library of Congress Catolog Card Number 95-083642
ISBN 1-883926-06-8
For permission to reproduce selections from this book,
write to:
Belle Grove Publishing Co.
P.O. Box 483, Kearny, N.J. 07032

Table of Contents

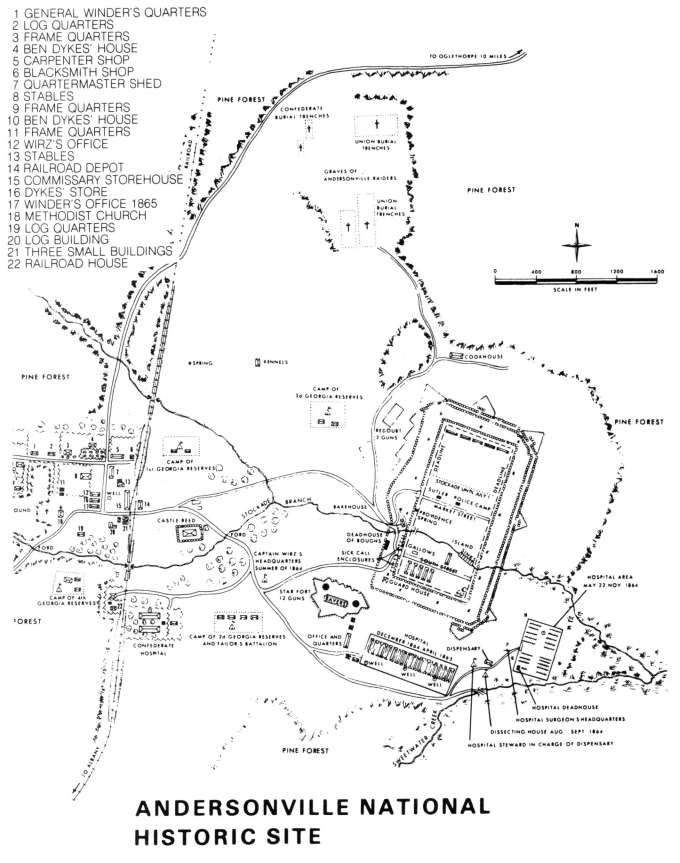

KEY TO BUILDINGS
IN AND ADJACENT TO ANDERSONVILLE

1 GENERAL WINDER'S QUARTERS
2 LOG QUARTERS
3 FRAME QUARTERS
4 BEN DYKES' HOUSE
5 CARPENTER SHOP
6 BLACKSMITH SHOP
7 QUARTERMASTER SHED
8 STABLES
9 FRAME QUARTERS
10 BEN DYKES' HOUSE
11 FRAME QUARTERS
12 WIRZ'S OFFICE
13 STABLES
14 RAILROAD DEPOT
15 COMMISSARY STOREHOUSE
16 DYKES' STORE
17 WINDER'S OFFICE 1865
18 METHODIST CHURCH
19 LOG QUARTERS
20 LOG BUILDING
21 THREE SMALL BUILDINGS
22 RAILROAD HOUSE

ANDERSONVILLE NATIONAL HISTORIC SITE

Foreword

"Down by the branch, at any time of the day or night, men by the score could be found dead or dying. They would crawl as near to the water as they could get, and then, being too weak to get over the filth that bordered and blocked the stream, would give up in despair, after trying in vain to reach the water; being too exhausted to go back where they started from they would, after terrible suffering, give up the ghost."

-- Harry Harman, 12th N.Y. Cavalry
Andersonville survivor.

Between February, 1864 and April, 1865 it is estimated that 45,000 Union prisoners were confined in the Confederate stockade, Camp Sumter, near Anderson Station, Georgia, forever to be remembered as Andersonville. Of that number, approximately 25,000 men survived their prison experience and returned home to tell their tale of suffering. It is unknown how many survivors, with their health and lives shattered, died as a direct result of their captivity after returning to civilian life. Close to 13,000 Union soldiers did "give up the ghost" in Andersonville, and it was the ghost of Andersonville that haunted the survivors for the rest of their lives.

By examining the existing written material on Andersonville, it can be seen that only a small percentage of prisoners ever formally recorded their experiences on paper. A select few of those prisoner accounts became well-known, best-selling books, while others were lesser-known pamphlets, sold by the veteran pensioners for only a few cents. However the vast majority of Andersonville survivors' reminiscences were written not for financial gain, but as letters that appeared in the various veteran newspapers that flourished after the war, such as **The National Tribune** and **The Grand Army Scout & Soldiers Mail**. Many of these letters were written as a response to a particular article while others simply related a survivors personal experience. Some of the letters are tinged with bitterness, and some with forgiveness. Others emotionally describe a painful prison memory such as the details of a comrade's death whose fate would be otherwise unknown to his distraught family.

One can only wonder what was the motivation for each man to write about his hellish experience. Perhaps, for some, it was therapeutic. Today, psychologists would consider this as an effective way to cope with "Post-Traumatic Stress Syndrome."

This book gathers a wide variety of prisoner writings including survivors' letters, memoirs, sketches, as well as the diaries of three prisoners; William F. Keys, 142nd Pennsylvania Infantry; George Hitchcock, 21st Massachusetts Infantry; and Samuel Melvin, 1st Massachusetts Heavy Artillery. The diaries are vital to help understand the day-to-day misery, monotony, and despair in Andersonville.

May this book serve as a tribute and remembrance to the Union soldiers who were held prisoner at Andersonville, and all American POWs.

William Styple
Kearny, N.J.
February, 1996

Escape from Andersonville by Walton Taber.

Part One
"I was among the first."

Memoirs of H. Clay Hartwell

H. CLAY HARTWELL
Battery A, 1st Michigan Light Artillery
Captured at Chickamauga, September 19, 1863.
Entered Andersonville on February 24, 1864.

I was among the first 400 who were sent to Andersonville from Belle Isle. When we got there the stockade was not completed, almost the entire end on the north side was covered with stumps, logs, limbs, brush--the debris from cutting the timber for the stockade. This was a bonanza for the boys, who had been all winter on the island without clothing, blankets, shelter, or fire, and the gate had hardly closed upon us before a fire was started, and if ever there was a "welkin ring" in the winds of Georgia it went up there and lasted as long as we had breath. Some of the most provident of our number saw a "glorious opportunity" to better their condition, and wisely gathered together enough of the logs, sticks, and limbs to make themselves very comfortable quarters, and retained them during their sojourn there. The stockade itself was built of square timbers, averaging about fifteen inches square. A trench was dug about six feet deep, a log fully a foot through was put in the bottom and these square timbers placed upright on this, leaving them about twenty feet above the ground. At this time a Colonel [Alexander W.] Persons, with his regiment , the Fifty-fifth Georgia--who, with his regiment, had been captured and paroled by our forces and then sent by the rebel authorities to guard the prison, was in charge of the stockade, and I must say that he was a gentleman. Well, we had not been in the stockade more than two or three days before there was not wood enough inside the pen to cook a cup of corn coffee with. True, individuals had gathered together quite a quantity of timber, limbs, and chips, but this was their private property, and the good-natured colonel allowed them to hold it as such, and would let as many of the boys go outside for wood as he could furnish guards to take care of. But this leniency presented a greater temptation than some of the boys could resist, so they struck for liberty and home by "mugging" the guard. This the colonel could not stand, so he finally shut down on the detail, and the boys began at once to devise other means of escape. The stockade was completed about the 20th of March, 1864. The guard was stationed on a small platform near the top of the stockade from the first, and about the 1st of April they built a sentry box, about four feet square, of rough pine boards, open in the front, from which they could look down on the inside.

As soon as the stockade was finished, we had "full swing" within the enclosure, the guards paying no attention to us, and a great many of the boys built their "shebangs" by the side of the stockade, which was a great help, as building material was scarce. Everything was going along in "apple pie" order. The colonel was obliging, the guards had tasted a little of prison life themselves, and were very clever towards us. Rations were abundant and of the best quality and fair variety, but not withstanding, there were restless spirits among the crowd, and they did not see why they should quietly "hang around there," with only a twenty-foot wall between them and freedom. I do not say as to boast, but I was one of those who caused the dead-line to be erected at Andersonville, as I was one of a party of thirteen who scaled the stockade on the night of March 24. On the southwest side of the stockade the timbers had settled, and in doing so quite large cracks were made between them, and we fingered and toed our way up and let ourselves down on the outside. We did not make very much progress towards escaping, however, for we were "gobbled" up about 9 o'clock the next morning, but the excitement of the undertaking and the experience was worth all of our disappointment. The vigilance of the guards was increased, and so was our determination to get away. The rebels did not disturb us in our quarters close to the stockade, and as my mess of eight had a very cozy shebang I thought it advisable not to run too much risk, or to scare the rebels into ordering us into other quarters, so I joined my fortunes with a party who were digging a tunnel very near the place where we had climbed over the stockade, because they thought the chances more favorable of getting under than over the wall. We put in nearly three weeks of hard work on the tunnel, and at last everything was completed and lots were drawn to determine in what order we should go out. There were only five of us in the working of the scheme, but, when we found it was a sure thing, we let about twenty-five into the secret, and this brought on the first trouble.

As soon as they knew of it they insisted in sharing an equal chance of getting away, instead of giving us, who had done all the labor, the first chance, so we had to compromise by drawing lots. My number on the roll was nineteen. We were to divide into squads of five as soon as we were fairly outside, and each party was to take a different route. All succeeded in getting beyond the guard safely, but not a soul succeeded in getting through to "God's country." It was while our pursuers were picking us up--two or three at a time--that Colonel Persons was relieved, and Wirz took command, or rather had charge and care of the guard around the stockade and the interior of the same, being responsible to General John H. Winder, who had followed the last of the prisoners from Richmond, and held the position of commissary-general of prisoners of war. The reasons assigned at the time for removing Col. Persons were that our Government had entered a protest against his doing guard duty, as it was in violation of the terms of parole. There was a great activity among the boys about this time and the writer and those connected with him in schemes of escape were not the only ones who were on liberty bent. Nearly every man was busy with some project in that direction. During the time we were being gathered in from our hiding places others had effected an escape over the stockade, but had been immediately discovered, and measures had been at once taken to prevent such occurrences in the future. I happened to be brought in to Wirz's headquarters about the same time that Sergeant Pritchie, of the Second Maryland, and a squad who had jumped over the stockade were brought up there. Wirz was swearing and storming wildly, and Winder was red hot with rage to think that any Marylander would fight for the ---- Yankees. I was personally pointed out to Wirz by the rebel sergeant, Emerson, as the man who had led the escapade a short time before, and was very forcibly reminded by old Wirz that I would be taken care of in the future. He kept his word by ordering me taken to the blacksmith's shop, where they attached a ball and chain, weighing about seventy pounds, to my ankles. The next day I was put back into the stockade, and found my comrades engaged in tearing down and moving our "shebang" away from the side of the stockade, while a force of men was following them up, driving stakes about four feet long into the ground and nailing on the top of them a narrow strip of board, which was christened "the dead-line."

The rebels did not fully agree among themselves as to the reasons why it was erected. Wirz said it was to get us so far away that the guard could readily see what we were doing all the time, as well as to prevent us climbing over the stockade and make it more difficult for us to dig tunnels. Winder said it was because rebel prisoners in our hands were subjected to the same treatment. Whatever were the true reasons of its inception, this is how it came to be erected. I wore the ball and chain about three weeks, when I succeeded in getting it off, and finally threw it into the filth at the lower end of the creek. I afterwards became better acquainted with old Wirz, but he never tried the ball and chain again on me. I was cognizant of a great many attempts of escape while at Andersonville, and never knew of my own knowledge, or heard from any reliable authority, that anybody ever succeeded in getting through to our lines from there. I was one of about seventy-five who made the break on the night of September 10th. I was retaken on the fourth day, forty miles west of Andersonville and taken back there again. There were five in my party, and all were recaptured.

Private George Weiser
Co. A, 10th New Jersey Infantry

Part Two
"Do you men ever expect to get out of this prison alive?"

Memoirs of George Weiser

PRIVATE GEORGE WEISER
Company A, 10th New Jersey Infantry, Sixth Corps.
Born in Germany in 1835. Enlisted on September 10, 1861.
Captured at Spotsylvania Court House, May 14, 1864.
Arrived in Andersonville, May 25, 1864.

Andersonville Stockade or Prison Pen was a pen of about sixteen acres of land, without shelter of any kind except two pine trees that stood in the Northern part of the Prison. Those two trees were cut down on or about the first of July. Wood was so scarce in the Prison we had to take the trees to do our cooking.

What little shelter we had was what the prisoners made themselves with their blankets, clothing or what ever they happened to have when they entered the prison. The Rebs gave us nothing for shelter.

This Prison Pen was enclosed by a Stockade of pine logs sixteen feet long set close together, four feet in the ground, or twelve feet above the ground, or twelve feet high, with two gates, both gates being on one side of the prison, one gate at the upper and one at the lower end, with a drive way so that a horse and wagon could come in and drive about half-way across the prison and turn.

The Reb guard had little sheds about twenty yards apart all the way around the Stockade; these sheds where made a little higher than the Stockade so that the guards could stand in them and watch the Prisoners.

These sheds where on the outside above the stockade. On the inside all the way around was the dead line, and it was certain death for any one who dared to cross the dead line; this line was on the inside of the Stockade or Prison Pen, it was thirty feet from each side and end, and was marked by a small railing nailed on top of stakes driven in the ground and about two feet high. This railing did not last long for the men being always short of wood, it was carried away piece at a time until it was gone, and there was nothing left to mark this dead line.

This was very bad for the new prisoners coming in, for those in the prison never told them about the dead line, and very often when fresh prisoners would come in they would rush over the dead line for a place to rest and some one would be sure to be killed or wounded before they could find out their mistake.

Through the center of this Prison was a ditch of water about one foot deep and three feet wide. About one third of this ditch at one end was used for a sink. This sink was marked by a railing, but by the first of July the railing, had all been used for wood to cook with. One-third of this ditch about midway was used to wash in and there could be seen hundreds of men there day and night waiting for their turn to wash themselves; I never washed in the ditch. One end of the ditch was used for drink water.

The Rebs had a cook house on the outside near the ditch, and much of the dirt from their cook house would get in the water, which made it very bad to drink. I never drank water from the ditch. At the end of the ditch inside of the dead line was a small running spring of water. The water would run out of this spring into the ditch and many of the men would reach through or under the dead line so as to get pure water, and there could be seen hundreds of men waiting for their turn to get water there, for only one or two at a time could get water in this way. There was so much danger that I never went there for water; too near the dead line for me.

There were about sixteen wells of water in this prison. These wells were from three to thirty feet deep but they were owned by private parties. Some of these wells would have as many as a hundred owners. We had nothing to dig these wells with; we had to dig them with our knives, tin cups and tin plates. It would take us three or four weeks to dig a well and some of the men would dig for weeks and find no water. I have seen men lowered down in these wells, twenty-five or thirty feet deep, with a leather string made from or out of a shoe. Any one who was not an owner was not allowed to use this well water, without they bought it at the rate of one cent a quart.

We had no pennies in this prison, and so when we wanted to buy water we would give one teaspoonful of corn meal, or one teaspoonful of mush or a chew of tobacco about the size of half a grain of corn. I was one of the owners of a well. The well that I had a share in was fifteen feet deep and it had eighteen owners and the water was good, we used this water to drink, to cook with, and to wash ourselves with. The owners of the wells had to watch over them day and night.

On both sides of the ditch the ground was low and muddy; the mud in some places was knee deep. The men could not stay on this low land. All who tried to live there would soon get sick and die. This low muddy ground contained about three acres. From this low land up to the stockade the ground was higher and it was between the dead line and the low land where the Prisoners lived. I have seen men in this low muddy ground up to their knees in the mud hunting for wood; every stump and every piece of wood was gathered and used for fuel to cook with.

This low muddy ground was used by the sick men who could not reach or get to the sink or ditch. In fact, many of the men were so sick that they could not walk down to the low land, and they had to dig little holes in the ground, and after using them they would cover them over, and these holes, thousand of them, would get full and by the effect of the hot sun and rain they would boil over and run down the hill. This was the cause of creating millions of maggots, and when we would lay down to sleep hundreds of these maggots would crawl over us. Some of them would crawl in our ears and in our mouths.

The Rebs gave us nothing for shelter so we had to depend on our own resources, or whatever we would happen to have when we entered the prison, and there were thousands of little shanties or tents of all description from a shelter tent to a hole in the ground. Many of the men had no shelter. They of course would soon be taken sick and die. There was a place in this prison we called the Island. It was a small neck of land that was very nearly surrounded by the low muddy ground. This island was near the center of the prison. It was on this island that I and a number of my friends located. There was about six hundred prisoners on this island, and about three hundred of them were from New Jersey. The men had no change of clothing and no soap to wash with, and living in so much dirt it was no wonder that all of the men in prison became lousy. We had to take our clothes off every day and hunt and kill the lice and nits. These were what we called body lice; we did not make much account of head lice. We had to kill the lice or they would kill us. Oh, pity the sick who could not or had not the strength enough to hunt their lice. The ground or sand seemed to be full of these lice and at any time we could see them crawling on us from off the ground.

I would like here to make a statement in regard to myself. From the fourth of July until the first day of September, every day in those two months, I killed three hundred lice and nits. When I got up to this number I would stop killing until the next day.

All the clothes I had was a hat, a coat, one pair of pants, one shirt, one pair of stockings and one pair of shoes. The first night that I landed in the prison I slept out in the open air. The next morning one of the prisoners had a board which he offered to sell for two dollars; it was an inch board twelve feet long and about ten inches wide, and Phil. Hilyard, of Williamstown, N.J.; Jacob Kay, of Longacoming, N.J.; George MacIntosh of Mauch Chunk, Pa., and I, made up the two dollars and bought the board. I put in twenty cents, all the money I had. With this board we made a frame for our shanty or tent and enclosed it with mud and clay which we dug from the low and muddy ground.

This shanty or tent was one foot high at the back, three feet high at the front, four feet long and four feet wide. Phil had a wool blanket that we used for an awning on the front toward the south. It was built for four, but when we got it finished only three could crawl in at a time, but it done very well to keep the hot sun off. We were raised in the North and this was so far South we suffered much by the heat. Every time it rained very much the roof of our shanty would get soft and fall in and part of the shanty would fall down, so we had the pleasure of building it up about once or twice a week. The shanty or tent of ours was called one of the best in prison and many of the men would come and take a drawing of it when they wanted to build. Oh, pity those who had no shelter, for there were thousands of them who had nothing to keep them from the hot sun and rain. About ten feet from our tent was the low muddy ground, and about five feet from the low land was where we dug our well of water.

When I was first put in this Prison Pen the men received their food ready cooked, of which, each one of us received half a pound of corn meal bread, and four ounces of boiled ham or bacon for one day's food. One day in each week we received four ounces of fresh beef. In addition to this we received every two days a half a pint of mush, or a half a pint of cooked beans, or six teaspoonfuls

Private Jesse Adams
Co. F, 10th New Jersey Infantry
Captured at Spotsylvania Court House, Va.
Died in Andersonville, Aug. 2, 1864. Grave #4581

of molasses; so you see part of the time we received two different kinds, and part of the time three kinds of food.

Well we went on at this rate until June the first, new prisoners coming in every day or two, until we numbered about twenty thousand, and it took so much food that the Rebs could not cook it for us, and some times it would be near sundown before we would receive anything to eat. The mush was put in large dry goods boxes; three or four of these boxes were filled with hot mush, put on a two horse open wagon, which the Rebs would drive into the prison. It took several of these boxes of mush to supply us, and some times the men would get tired waiting, and when the loaded wagon would come in, many of the men would make a raid on the wagon, upset the boxes and spill the mush; in this way it would get wasted and many of the men had to go without mush that day.

The Rebs and the prisoners soon got tired of this, so we had two companies of regulators of police appointed. It was the duty or work of the regulators to keep the raiders from the food wagons, for which service they received double rations. The Rebs said that they could not cook our corn meal bread for us so now they gave us our corn meal raw and wood to cook all our food except the mush, beans, rice and molasses. Generally these articles were cooked before we got them, but some times we would receive them raw. We received our ration of food about in this way: Sunday we received corn meal, saltmeat and half a pint of cooked rice; Monday, corn meal and saltmeat; Tuesday, corn meal, saltmeat and a half pint of mush; Wednesday, corn meal, and fresh beef; Thursday, corn meal, saltmeat and six teaspoonfuls of molasses; Friday, corn meal and saltmeat; Saturday, corn meal, saltmeat and half a pint of cooked beans, and then on Sunday, corn meal, etc.

This is, or was, about the way they tried to feed us during the nine months that I was there. We had four separate days we received no food, twice we received no food for three days at a time, about thirty days we received no meat, and we received no mush, rice, beans or molasses for forty days at a time. These days we received nothing but corn meal and meat. When we commenced to get our food raw, it was on or about the first of June and from that time we had to do the cooking ourselves. At first we received one quart of corn meal and four ounces of meat for one day's food.

This was more corn meal than many of the men could eat, for there were many sick who did not eat one pint a day; I could eat my quart every day. Each man received a piece of wood about one inch square and three feet long every day to cook with. This wood was too small to do our cooking with and as soon as it burned out we would eat our food, very often, half cooked. We went on in this way for about three weeks. The sick did not eat their full ration of food. Corn meal was plenty, we could buy it in any part of the prison for five cents a quart. I kept about four quarts on hand. Many of the men would try to keep their meal but it would get wet and sour, and corn meal could be seen all through the prison where the men had thrown it away.

The Rebs saw this and they thought that they were giving us too much to eat, so in the last week in June our food was cut down one-half. The next day after food was cut down, corn meal went up to fifty cents a quart and never sold for less during my imprisonment. I never received salt from the Rebs while in Andersonville prison. I do not think that they ever gave the prisoners any salt except what was in the meat.

The price of salt was five cents a tablespoonful or fifty cents a pint. It was now the first of July

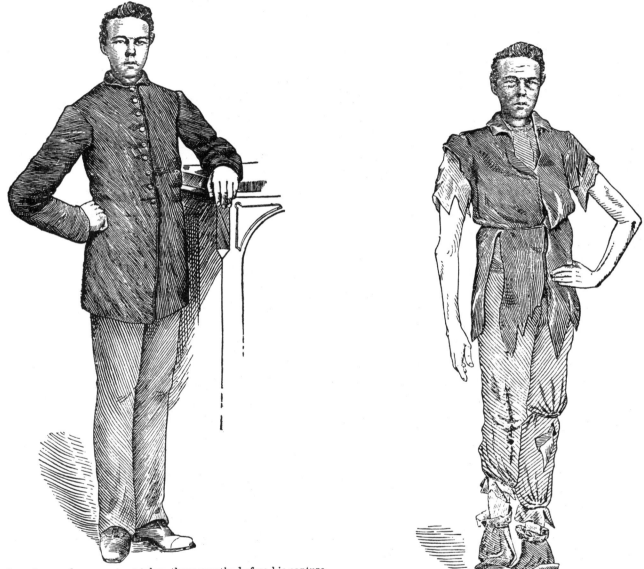

The Author, from a daguerreotype taken three months before his capture.

The author just before he made his escape.

Portraits taken from
Nine Months in Rebel Prisons
By George Weiser

and new prisoners were coming in and we numbered about thirty thousand. At this time we were pested with a gang of our men who were called Mosby's Raiders. There seemed to be about one thousand of these men banded together, nearly all of them were known, and we could point them out wherever we would see them. These men, or raiders did not disturb many of the old prisoners but they would steal off of the new ones when they first came in, which made a great deal of trouble in the prison.

One day three Rebs came in the prison. One appeared to be a doctor who had a little pet dog with him. I saw one of the raiders slip up behind them and steal the dog. He took it to his shanty, killed it and made it into soup. I saw that same raider that evening going through the prison selling soup. He would sing out, "here is your nice mutton soup, twenty-five cents a pint, with a piece of mutton in every pint." The doctor never knew what became of his dog. One day these raiders stole a watch. Some said they stole from the Rebs and some said they stole it off of one of the new prisoners. I do not know which it was for when any thing happened in the prison we could hear all kind of rumors; any way there was quite a riot started on account of it.

The watch was never found but the raiders got themselves into trouble by it. The excitement was so strong that the Rebs marched in a company of their men. They then had it explained to them how we were tormented by the raiders. The captain in charge of the prison now ordered the regulators to arrest all the raiders and send them outside to him. The regulators in two days had arrested over three hundred and sent them out. They were then tried by a court-martial composed of prisoners and rebels, six of them were found guilty of murder. One of their shanties was dug out and one of the prisoners found murdered and buried therein. Then all but the six where sent back into the prison again and they were kept out until the eleventh of July.

The Captain that had charge over the prison came in and said, "we have arrested some of your men and have given them a fair trail; six of them have been found guilty of murder; we do not know what to do with those six men; they ought to be hung, but we dare not hang them for fear your government may retaliate, so we have made up our minds to send them back into the prison and let them go. You men can take them, let them go free, hang them or do what you like with them." Every thing had been still and silent while the captain was speaking, but now a cry went up from five thousand men, to "hang them;" "hang them."

One of the prisoners went up to the captain in charge of the prison and said that he would hang them if the captain would give him lumber to build a scaffold and rope to do the hanging with, for, said he, "these raiders have killed my brother and I want to hang them for it." The captain said he would send every thing in that was needed. A wagon was sent in with the lumber and soon the men had a scaffold built with six ropes dangling on it. Then about three o'clock in the afternoon the six men were brought in hand-cuffed. The captain in charge of the prison then removed the hand-cuffs and turned the men over to the prisoners. The Rebs then all went out except the Quartermaster and the Priest. These two stayed inside the prison until after the hanging. There were about five thousand prisoners at this time standing crowded together near the gate.

As soon as the six men where relieved of their cuffs one of them, the leader of the gang, made a break for liberty. He ran through this crowd of five thousand men, up and down the prison, across the low muddy ground, went up to his knees in mud, fell down, crawled out of the mud, got on the up land and kept on running until some one run up to him and caught him. Then they were taken to the scaffold, the ropes put around their necks, mealsacks pulled over their heads, and soon they were dangling in the air. One man broke the rope but he was put up again and hung. They were left hanging for about one hour when a wagon drove in and they were then cut down, loaded on the wagon and took out. This stopped the raiding and there was no raiders now to be found. Now if a man was caught stealing he was taken to the regulators and if found guilty, he was tied to a post, received from five to twenty lashes, and then let go.

Now in regards to drawing or dividing our rations or food. In every detachment or thousand men there was one Reb and one Union man appointed over them. It was the work of the Reb to count his thousand every morning. This was done by counting the first, second, third, and so on hundred at a time. Then the Reb would report to the Rebel Quartermaster, draw the rations or food, and turn it over to the Union man that had charge of the thousand. This Union man would then divide the food into ten parts for which service he would receive a double rations of food. Each hundred had one Union man appointed over them and it was the work of this man to draw the rations for his men from the man that had charge of the thousand. Then this man would divide the food into four parts for which he would receive for his work a double ration or two shares of food; and one Union man had charge over the mess, or twenty-five men. It was the work of this man to draw the portion of food for the twenty-five men and divide it and for this work he received nothing. It was the rule for the man that divided the twenty-five to always take the last ration; this rule caused him to divide it very true and exact; every man seemed to get his full share. When we received fresh beef with a bone in it the bone would count for one ration of meat as any of the men would take it in preference to the meat. One man told me that he had boiled his beef bone forty times, always getting a little substance out of it to season his corn meal or meal cake. At one time the man that was in charge of my mess of twenty-five got sick and died. I was appointed to divide the rations, and the first day I was short of one ration of meat. Of course I had to go without meat for that day. I divided the rations for two or three weeks; I soon found that I was losing in strength so I threw up the job and some one else took it.

It was surprising to see the large amount of food it took every day to feed the prisoners, and when it was divided we would only have about half enough to eat. I have seen ten barrels of molasses carted into prison for one day's ration and when it was divided to thirty-five thousand men it was only six teaspoonfuls to each man. It took more than five hundred bushels of corn meal every day to feed those men, each man receiving only one pint of corn meal. It took five or six thousand pounds of meat every day and all we received was about three ounces of meat a day for each man. It took twelve or fifteen cords of wood every day and when it was divided out to each man it would not make enough fire for cooking. We had many different ways of preparing our food to eat. One way we ate the mush was to put cold water on it, then shut our eyes and imagine that we were eating mush and milk. I ate my mush often in this way and then told the men that it was hard to tell water from milk. We had many ways in using molasses; some would drink it as soon as they got it, others would trade it off for four or five teaspoonfuls of meal or a little piece of meat. Hundreds of the men had nothing to put the molasses in and they would get it in the top of their caps, or in an old rag, or in their hands. These poor fellows would have to eat theirs very quickly or loose or waste it. Some of the men would trade all their corn meal and meat for molasses; out of the molasses they would make candy, sell it and then take the money and buy something else to eat.

I always divided my ration or food into two meals; I eat one in the afternoon or evening and the other in the morning. I had a quart tin cup and a tin plate, that I cooked in; everyday I had what I called Coffee. I took four or five teaspoonfuls of corn meal, put it in the tin plate, put the plate over the fire and burn the meal black; then I put the burnt meal in the tin cup with one pint of water and brought it to a boil. This made very good coffee and when I drank the coffee I always ate the grounds so that nothing would be lost. I would make the corn meal out in a little water into two cakes and bake them in my tin plate over the fire; some times I would cut my meat in small pieces, mix it with the corn meal and bake it altogether; this making the cake very good and rich. When I received fresh beef I always made a cup of soup and put corn meal dumplings in it. I was in these prison pens nine months and was sick one day, so I had a fair chance to see much that was going on in the prison.

And now it was July fifteenth, and new prisoners were still coming in, and the cry was, "still they come." The Prison Pen had become so full of men, that the Rebs had it enlarged, and now we had about twenty-four or five acres of land in our prison.

Our food began to get short; the overplus was all used up and now what food we received would do very well for the sick to die on, but it was far to small for healthy men to live on.

Save us! oh, save us! what shall we do. New prisoners coming in every day until the number ran up to forty thousand, with about half enough to eat, and the cry was "what shall we do" or "what will we do." There were the men that had been the bravest of the Country, who had stood before the enemy in the heat of battle and fought until they were wounded or captured, but now they are so reduced and starved that their hearts sink, their strength is gone, and they are passing away forever. There was nothing in this prison pen but famine and danger.

The men were wild with torment; they looked one another in the eyes and wept. Some swore and some cried, some went mad, many were sickly and many died. It had not rained for several days and the prison was filthy from one end to the other, death was staring every man in the face. The Rebs too got uneasy. They planted a battery of artillery on the outside at each corner of the prison and threatened to blow us all into eternity sooner than let us escape. About this time a thunderstorm arose and the lightning struck in many places all about the prison, the rain descended in mighty power flooding all of the low land of the prison. The water made the ground so soft that both ends of the Stockade where it crossed the low land fell down and the water rushed through carrying all the filth and dirt with it.

And now it was in August and the men's clothing began to give out; some had only a pair of pants, some only a shirt, some drawers, some only had a cap, some a pair a shoes, many were barefooted, and many nearly naked. We had a mass meeting and elected three of our men to go Washington, D.C. and see if they could make some terms for us to get away.

The Rebs said they would send the three men through the lines. The three men went off and that was the last we ever seen of them. The Rebs said that they would never exchange a black for a white one, and that was the only terms our Government would exchange on, so there would be no exchange until the war was over.

In July and August we had about six thousand sick men in the prison, about three thousand of whom where almost helpless and dying. The dead averaged about one hundred a day and one day we had two hundred and four deaths. Every day the dead were carried out to the dead house by four of his friends. We had a sick call every day at ten o'clock. This call was at the gate where the doctor would come in and look at the sick. I will explain the sick call: At ten o'clock a drummer boy would come in near the gate and beat the drum, about three thousand of the sick would then start for the gate and about three hundred would hold out to reach there, the rest of the men would all give out before they got near the gate and they would hear, "the sick call is over" and they had to get back to their shanties the best they could.

A great many of these men had their friends to help them; these too would start to answer the sick call. Each one would have three or four friends who would pick them up and start for the gate; some of these were carried in blankets, some on sticks of wood and some on shoulders of their friends, each party trying to rush their man in ahead of the other. Some of these would run into each other, throw down their men and fight for the right of way. Very often when the fight was over one or the other of the sick men would be dead. This surely was a sad sight. About three hundred would reach the gate, and carried up in this way, it took a long time to reach there for our motion was very slow, we had been so reduced that we could not move fast.

The sick are at the gate near the dead-line--that is all that were able to get there--about six or seven hundred and these hope to get medicine; two doctors come in and look at them, pick out three or four and send them out to the hospital, the doctors then give a little red root or a few pills to about fifty of the sick men, and then the doctor says "that's all we can do" and tell the men to come again to-morrow; then the men are taken back to their holes and shanties again disappointed and dying.

Sometimes the sick would be waiting for the doctor and word would come that he would not be in today, and some of the men would give up all hope and die.

There was a great deal of trade and traffic carried on in this prison and there seemed to be about forty thousand dollars in greenbacks, or United States money, in circulation. Some of the prisoners would have as low as five cents and some as high as one hundred dollars. This money was all the time in circulation, and some of it would get so black and dirty that we could scarcely tell the value of it. All of the currency or small notes less than a dollar were kept in the prison; these we used for retail trade. There was many thousand men in this prison who never had a cent of money of any kind while they were in there. I was with the number without money while in this prison. Oh pity the poor, and the sick who had no money. The rebs allowed the farmers to sell to the prisoners but they were not allowed to enter the prison, neither were they allowed to sell for greenbacks. The prisoners that bought off these farmers had to be escorted out of the prison under guard to buy their produce, so every day there would be a few prisoners taken out to buy goods, and some of the prisoners would stand at the gate for weeks at a time waiting for their turn. Many of them never got out for it was just who happened to be the lucky one, so those that got out would buy for those that did not. The Reb farmer was not allowed to sell for greenback so the prisoners had to buy Rebel money. Some how or another there was always plenty of this Reb or Confed money in the prison and for sale by the prisoners. How this money got into the prison or how the prisoners got possession of it I do not know. When we wanted to buy we would just call out, "whose got Confed to sell," and in five minutes we would see some of the prisoners coming to us with their hands full of it. The greatest mystery of all was the way this Reb money was sold. We always got five dollars of Confed money for one dollar in greenbacks, and some times we could get six for one, seven for one, and I have seen the time when we could get ten for one, and very likely the next day it would be five for one.

We always judged how things where going on in the outside world by the rise and fall of this money. We always got twenty dollars in Confed for one in gold. The buying and selling on the inside of the prison was all done with United States money. The money would have soon all disappeared if it had not been for new prisoners coming in. Some of these men would have five, ten or twenty dollars each and in one week's time their money would be gone. Many of them would start little stores or shebangs and make out to live for weeks and months. If a man had a dollar he was called rich, but if he had no money he was called poor. I was between the two for I was part owner of a good well of water which threw me in with both classes. There were many stores in this prison and they were rated from one dollar up to twenty. If a man had a barrel he started a beer saloon and his fortune was made; all he done was to throw in corn meal and water and dip out sour beer for five cents a pint. There were three of these saloons in the prison. Tin cups and kettles were one dollar for a quart one, four dollars for a four quart kettle. These tin cups and kettles were made out of old tin that the prisoners gathered up on their way to prison and there was always ready sale for all the old tin that came in; this tin was found along the railroads where wrecks had happened. There was also a shop for repairing watches and jewelry in the prison and the men that worked in it made out well. Every man was considered lucky who made enough to buy his salt and a few extra mouthfuls of food to eat. There were four or five barber shops; shaving ten cents, hair cutting ten cents.

There were four or five hundred colored prisoners in this prison and nearly all of them were lame or wounded. Theirs was a sad fate indeed, some of them said that they had been wounded after they were captured. All the prisoners seemed to be affected with the scurvy; many were broke out in black spots and some were so bad that their teeth fell out, many were so bad that they would swell up to twice their size and the black spots would break and burst out, and large gangrene sores would eat the flesh from their bones, and I often seen the bare bones through the sores for many days before the men were dead. Many of the men were troubled with the diarrhea, many died from this cause. The corn meal did not agree with them and they had no way to cure themselves. The men were troubled much with fever; some would be taken and die soon, this we called the yellow fever and some would be taken and linger long, this kind we called the slow fever. They were so reduced that their hip bones had nothing on them but the thin skin and sometimes they would get so sore that we could see the bone. This made the men sleep in all ways. Most of the time in this prison I slept in a sitting position with my knees drawn up and my head and arms resting on my knees. I remember one day standing at the dead line near the gate, it was about the time of the sick call and I was standing there counting the dead that had been brought up to the gate that morning, seventy-eight in number, but they had not yet been carried out to the dead house, and the prison seemed to have on all of its

Corporal Philip Hilyard
Co. A, 10th New Jersey Infantry
Captured at Spotsylvania, Va., May 14, 1864
Died in Andersonville, Sept. 3, 1864. Grave #7900

agony when I looked up and saw six women looking over the top of the stockade, and I heard one of them remark, "I have often wondered why the Confederacy did not succeed but now I know; no nation can prosper who does a thing like this," and the women turned from the sight.

While in this prison I had many dreams and I often dreampt of going home and setting at the table filled with plenty of good things to eat. I dreampt this so often that one night when I was in a dream sitting at the table with my brother and sisters and every thing seemed to be full and plenty, when I said, "there is no use of my eating because this is nothing but a dream. I have dreamed this often, I believe this too is not real." "Oh no," said my sister, "this is no dream. "See," said she, "take this hot cup of coffee and eat and drink for if this was a dream I could not hand you this." "Well," I said, "I will try it this time for surely this is no dream." So we had a good time eating and drinking but when I awoke I was very much disappointed for I was a thousand miles from home.

Many of the men tried to escape by tunnels, these tunnels were dug under ground, three or four feet deep and three or four hundred yards long. Not many of the prisoners ever made their escape in this way, the tunnel or hole only being large enough to permit one man to crawl out at a time, the Rebs would discover them before we could complete them.

And now it is the last week of August, we have had our hardest thunder storms in this month; it flooded the prison and washed off the filth and dirt; the ground was cold and damp and the men dying off by hundreds, the days were hot but the nights were chilly and all the men begs the Rebs to give them shelter for the sick. The Rebs sent us in two or three wagon loads of boards and we put up two sheds open in the front and closed in the back and ends, these sheds were only for the sick that was helpless which were thousands. Many of the sick men had nothing of any kind to cook with not even so much as a tin cup or a tin plate; many of the sick and well, both, were without anything to cook with for the Rebs gave us nothing to cook in and if the men could not borrow a tin cup or plate from their friends they had to eat their food raw. It was now the first of September, the sheds were completed and the sick was being carried to them. All that could walk was called well and all that could not walk was called sick, the four in my tent was able to walk up to this time. Kay was sick from eating raw meal, Hilyard was failing fast, MacIntosh and I were in good health. In the mud hole or tent behind my tent where three men lived, all were dead. The tent on the right side of my tent where two men lived, one was dead and the other one in good health. The tent on the left side of my tent where three men lived, two were dead and one in good health. This is the way things were about the first day of September, when we heard a strong rumor that the prisoners were going to be exchanged. About this time Phil Hilyard said to us, "do you men ever expect to get out of this prison alive?" I told him that I hoped to get out all right. He said that he was sure that he would die before he got home; he failed fast after this and at midnight on the third of September he died. Kay got so weak that he gave up all hope and said that he believed that he too would soon die. On the seventh of September the Rebs said we would be exchanged and they began to take the prisoners out of the prison. On the eighth of September we carried Kay up and put him in the shed; he was alive when I left the prison. On the ninth of September my old friend MacIntosh got uneasy and slipped out with another detachment and left me alone. On the tenth of September my detachment or thousand was ordered out. We were taken to the railroad and put in boxcars and started North. Now I was very sad indeed;

my three comrades gone, my clothes ragged and torn, I did not know what to do. I soon found two men that had lived along side of me and were in the same car with me, one of these men was Frank Beegle of the Fifteenth regiment, New Jersey Vol., and the other was Orlando Gallagher of my regiment. Both of the men had a wool blanket but I had none; we had only one blanket at our tent and when Phil got sick we sold it to get him something to eat, so these men said that I should go with them and that they would let me sleep in the middle. This was very good news indeed to me, but still I was sad to think that we had left so many behind. It is said that thirteen thousand died in Andersonville Prison Pen, but if each man had been truly counted the dead would number many more than fourteen, fifteen or even sixteen thousand.

Orlando Gallagher's partner that he had at Andersonville died and left him with a silver watch valued at fifty dollars. I had a gold ring worth about two dollars which I had not parted with. On the fifteenth of September we landed at a place called Florence, South Carolina. Here we were taken from the cars and put in a large field and a strong guard put over us. About eight or ten thousand prisoners had now arrived here and it was two days since we had eaten our last food. I now traded off my ring for a peck of sweet potatoes, Orlando bought some meat and corn meal, Frank hunted up some pieces of wood and we soon had a good feed. The Rebs said that they did not know that we were coming and that nothing had been prepared to feed us, so that night and the next day made three days since we had food. The men began to starve and die and we commenced to carry the dead up and lay them on the ground near the guards, some of the guards would say "what's the matter with that man." We would say that the man has starved to death and every one of us will starve to death if we are kept without food another day. The Rebs thought that there were some truth to this and they started out through the country and gathered up three or four wagon loads of corn cake and sweet potatoes; this was divided with the men and the next day the Rebs began to give us our corn meal and meat regular. It was in this place that I saw three men lay on the ground and crying, "o' for a spoonful of meal to save my life!" and the next morning I went to see if they were still there and there the three men lay cold and stiff in death.

George Weiser eventually made his escape near Wilmington, N.C. on February 22, 1865. He died in 1928.

Part Three
"Many were the fights for dead mans' rags."
Memoirs of Henry A. Harman

HENRY A. HARMAN
Troop A, 12th New York Cavalry
Captured at Plymouth, N.C., on April 20, 1864.

The first thing every morning the prisoners were ordered to fall into line, and were counted. This generally took an hour or two; on several occasions we were kept standing in ranks all day while the rebs tried to make their count come out all right, and agree with the number of rations that they were issuing. On these occasions orders were given to the guards to shoot any prisoner attempting to leave his place in line. Twice to my recollection they kept us in line this way all day, and without rations, and once they kept rations two days trying to find who the men were that flanked from one "ninety" to the other and drew double rations. They never issued any back rations, so we were out just so much, and no extra amount to make it up with.

Just imagine what this meant to us. We were on the verge of starvation when receiving "full" rations; then to be without entirely for 48 hours and fall back on the same amount as before.

From the south gate clear across the prison grounds ran a wide street, which by common consent was not encroached upon by any "shebang" or shelter. This was the main promenade, business street, and market combined. Here the rations were issued in bulk by the rebs to the Sergeants of the divisions, and here all the trading and gambling was done.

The street was generally lined by traders of all descriptions. The most that any one trader could show as his stock was a few beans, a sweet potato, half a teaspoonful of salt, and plug of tobacco, and perhaps an onion. Some would have the beans cooked, and would sell the soup. No matter in what style or shape you wanted any of the rations we received served up, there you could find it; and no matter what you had to trade, tobacco or grub, little or much, there you could find your man.

Among the traders were the gamblers, or "chuck-luck" men; they would sit all day with the boards across their knees, with figures from 1 to 6 marked upon them, inviting all to try their luck. You placed any amount you chose in cash on any figure represented and then shook the dice-box. If the figure you bet on came up you won the face of your stake, but if not you lost your stake.

There was considerable money floating around camp, and these "chuck-luck" men managed in the end to secure the most of it. This street was crowded at all times, and the cries of the different business men singing the praises of their goods, accompanied by those wanting to trade this for that, was deafening; but at 4 o'clock in the afternoon, when rations were issued, it was pandemonium indeed.

The personal appearance of the individuals of this crowd would be hard to describe. Begrimed with pitch-pine smoke of months, which water without soap could not be removed, and probably with the majority had not been tried; clothing of such scant quantity that shirt and drawers would be considered an extensive wardrobe; shoes and stockings a luxury that not one in a thousand could boast of. Take them as a whole, they were the most forlorn-looking lot of creatures that could be imagined.

Scattered among the crowd, and stretched out on the ground (not only here but all over the camp), were men in the last stages of disease, generally that of the bowels and other kindred complaints. As the coarse food that was issued to the prisoners only aggravated complaints of this kind, which were the most prevalent, the prisoners died by the hundreds. It was such a common occurrence to see men dying in all manner of places and conditions that it was looked upon with indifference and caused no remark; it was part and parcel of the place, and we had become so accustomed to it that we thought nothing of it.

Down by the branch at any time of the day or night men by the score could be found dead or dying. They would crawl as near to the water as they could get, and then, being to weak to get over the filth that bordered and blocked the stream, would give up in despair, after trying in vain to reach the water; being too exhausted to go back where they started from they would, after terrible suffering, give up the ghost.

The dead were picked up every morning, carried to the gate and laid out in a row, ready for the dead-wagon to draw them out. Very few bodies would be left with any clothing on them; it would be in the majority of cases be stripped from them before the breath had left the body.

Many were the fights for dead mens' rags. It was pitiable to view the naked dead as they were pitched like cord-wood into the wagon preparatory to their ride to the deadhouse or cemetery. They were thrown in indiscriminately. It was horrible to see the heads, arms and legs as they swung back and forth with the jolting motion of the wagon. This wagon was made to do double duty, for it not only carried the dead out in the morning, but it brought in our rations of bread in the afternoon, not as much as being swept out. As an appetizer I think this was a success, especially after noting the condition of the load in the morning, which certainly could be classed as perishable freight.

We had now, if not before, reached the deplorable condition where everything had to give way to the question of something to satisfy the continual cravings of an empty stomach. We cared for, talked of, and thought of nothing else. All schemes of trading with and fooling the guards had long since been given up as of no account. They had been accustomed to dealing with Yankees, and were not so green as of old. Furthermore every article we had to trade had vanished long since in the vain attempt to fill that aching void.

Everything centered on rations. The one thing we had to look forward to was rationtime. No sooner were rations received and swallowed than we commenced to count the hours until the next issue. The last thought at night was rations, congratulating ourselves in the morning that we were so much nearer the longed-for hour. As the moments slowly rolled away, our nerves by 2 o'clock would be wrought to an intense pitch. Excitement ran high, and a stranger would, if he could have looked upon us, have supposed that some great good fortune was about to be realized by the whole camp.

The time for issuing rations was 4 p.m. Long before 2 o'clock the majority of the prisoners would be anxiously and eagerly watching the road that led toward the kitchen, which lay out of sight, to the northwest of the stockade.

The first indication of the expected and longed-for load of "grub" would be the tip-ends of the mule's ears, which came into view above the intervening hilltop. Then a shout would go up from the camp, which, as the balance of the mules and wagons came into sight, was taken up by the whole body of inmates, and might have been heard miles away.

From the time rations were issued until dark, the prison presented a lively scene of trading, cooking, and hustling around generally, trying to make the most of the small ration that we received. Rations were issued alternately to half the camp raw one day, cooked the next.

One great and unnecessary privation was that of wood. The 35,000 prisoners who had been confined there had, before the Summer had half passed away, used every vestige of wood, even digging down several feet for the roots where the stumps of the trees had stood. The prison was surrounded by a dense pine forest, and nothing would have been easier than to give axes to squads under suitable guard daily to cut all the wood needed. So they were allowed to suffer for that which might have been so easily obtained.

It was a great deprivation even in Summer to have no wood to cook with, but now became much more so, when the weather was freezing cold. The little wood we obtained we were obliged to split into pieces the size of matches, and use it in that shape to do our cooking with. One man from every squad of 30 was allowed the privilege of going twice a week to the woods under guard and bringing back as much wood as he was capable of carrying, for the use of himself and of the other 29 of his squad. As the wood that could be picked up (no axes were allowed) had been pretty well cleaned up near the prison, we were obliged to go over a mile before finding any. The piece of wood that one man in our enfeebled condition could carry that distance would be small indeed; nevertheless, this was all we could get, and we had to be content. The idea of having a fire to get warm by was preposterous. Most of the time we had none to cook with.

In order to go on the wood squad we had to wait our chance at the gate, and days would often elapse ere anyone from our mess would be of the lucky number. It was not unusual for prisoners to have the life crushed out of them while waiting for a chance to go for wood.

At least one-third of the prisoners had absolutely nothing to draw or cook their rations in. These poor fellows, if the rations were cooked immediately devoured them as soon as received, and if raw, would trade them for stuff that was cooked, which they could generally do by paying a large percentage for the exchange. If no one would trade with them, they would eat the meal and beans as they were. Everything was toil that came to their mill; forever "snooping" around and eating stuff picked from all sorts of places.

Every time when we drew molasses a young fellow in our mess would invariably keep his rations until evening. When everybody else had devoured all the eatables that they had, then he would turn his molasses into a half a canteen and boil it leisurely over the fire. The aroma from the cooking molasses to hungry men was tantalizing to the extreme, and by the time that he had the stuff cooked to his satisfaction the boys sitting around were about wild in their regrets that they had not saved their own. After he had commenced to eat the candy the boys would begin to bid for it. One would offer to-morrow's ration of bread. No; he would decline to sell as yet. Finally, when the candy been nearly all eaten, he would sell the remainder for, say, half ration next day's bread. When the following day's rations were issued the man that bought the candy would be so much short of his regular allowance, and would generally anticipate his rations for the next day, and so on every day until the big interest he was paying for the accommodation in bread would swamp him, and he would have to live on almost nothing to pay his indebtedness.

Many were the ways of trying to get enough stuff ahead to have one square meal. I went into the soup business for a few days. I boiled a half-pint of buggy beans in two gallons of water, and went into the market on "Broadway," and sold a dish of soup for half-ration of beans, bread, or tobacco.

It required considerable strength of will to run the business long, and not turn to and devour the capital. I stuck to it for two days, and then, having sold the most of the water off the beans, I brought what was left home, and all in our mess had quite a satisfactory meal.

There was a sutler's store in the camp run by the rebs, but so far as the majority of the prisoners was concerned it might as well not have been there, for they had no money. In Confederate money bread cost $2; onions, $5 each; sweet potatoes, $40 per bushel. I don't believe there was Confederate money enough in camp to buy a five-pound bag of salt.

Tobacco was as hard to get as anything else; a quarter of my rations went daily for it. Although I never was accustomed to chewing until after entering Andersonville. I am satisfied that but for its use I should not have survived.

The site of Andersonville was on two side hills, a brook or branch running through the center. Along the branch above the prison the rebel troops were camped. All their refuse was thrown into the brook and floated down through the prison, and, as the stream was narrow and sluggish, the water was almost always unfit for use, even to wash in.

Under these circumstances, the procuring of water fit for cooking, etc., was almost an impossibility, as the only way that it could be got was by reaching far out under the dead-line, thereby inviting a shot from the guard on top of the stockade, not 30 feet away. There was, day or night, always such a crowd at this spot after water that it was only by the utmost exertion, and after waiting your chance for hours, that any could be had.

Such was the state of affairs up to Aug. 9, 1864, when something took place that was singular, and certainly providential. During a heavy thunder storm, some of the timbers of the stockade, alongside of the branch at the upper side of the camp, were washed loose, tearing away the embankment considerably. After the storm it was noticed that a beautiful, clear stream of water flowed from out the embankment. After the stockade was replaced this continued to run. As the spring was inside the dead-line, the rebs kindly put a trough in such a shape that it conveyed the water within the reach of the prisoners.   Although the stream was small it was continuous and cold.

In February, 1865, affairs in prison remained about the same.   No new prisoners had arrived in some time, and exchange talk was below par.   We had about come to the conclusion that we never would get out, except as we were carted out in the dead-wagon.   The death rate continued to increase; from 30 to 50 were taken to the trenches daily.

The rebel recruiting officers came in every day now, and offered all the old inducements and some new ones.   The rebs said that our Government had deserted us.   It certainly looked so, and in reality it had, as it was the policy to sacrifice the prisoners for the general good and the early close of the war. We knew that if we were exchanged, our Government would give able-bodied men, fit at once to go to the front, for poor starved creatures, who probably never be able to fight again.   Exchange would prolong the war indefinitely, and if necessary, be sacrificed for the preservation of the Union, rather than dishonor ourselves and our flag by taking the oath of allegiance to the Confederacy.

For the rest of his life, Henry A. Harman suffered ill health.   He died in 1893.

BREAKING AWAY OF THE STOCKADE BY THE FLOOD.

Photograph taken by A. J. Riddle on August 16, 1864 of prisoners gathered around the ration wagon on Broadway.

Part Four

"Death will soon be regarded as our best friend."

Diary of William F. Keys

SERGEANT WILLIAM FARRAND KEYS
Company K, 143rd Pennsylvania Infantry, Fifth Corps.
Age: 25.
Enlisted on August 21, 1862.
Captured in the Wilderness, May 5, 1864.
Arrived in Andersonville on May 23, 1864.

Monday, May 23, 1864. Reached Macon about noon and after a short delay pushed on for our destination sixty-three miles from there on the road to Americus. We ran down in about 3 hours and just before sunset entered the gates of the prison, nine hundred and ninety-one of us, swelling the number already there to about sixteen thousand. The place of our captivity in an enclosure of about five acres surrounded by stockades 15 feet high. A dirty stream runs through the middle of it and a piece of swamp lies along the eastern side of the stream. The ground is now all occupied except this swamp and the other margin of the stream.

Tuesday, May 24, 1864. Very hot. I went half way around the prison this morning and returned heart sick. Such sights as I have seen today these eyes never looked upon before. I have often read descriptions of misery and destitution drawn both from realities and imagination but nothing that I have ever read or dreamed or heard of comes up to what may be seen here any day or hour. Some of the prisoners have been here eight months and now scarcely a rag to cover their nakedness while starvation and disease have reduced them to living skeletons.

Wednesday, May 25, 1864. Hot. Nothing unusual transpiring. A few more Yanks came in today, they were captured near Spottsylvania Court House, some of them as late as the 14th inst. They report Meade as driving Lee steadily and that he has captured a great many prisoners. We also have information from the rebels themselves that Sherman has almost reached Atlanta having knocked

Johnston and his rebs quite "concave." A thunder shower this evening gave us a rather unpleasant foretaste of what we may expect in stormy weather.

Thursday, May 26, 1864. Warm. Some of the more irrepressible of these 15,000 captive Yanks have been meditating an escape, at least the thing has been talked over so that the rebel spies have got hold of it, and whether a plot exists or not they evidently fear it. They have had the niggers digging a trench today between the stockade and the "dead line" to discover the whereabouts of the supposed tunnel, but thus far they have found nothing. They scour the vicinity of the camp every morning with bloodhounds for fear some poor devil may have dug his way out of their pesthouse prison during the night.

Friday, May 27, 1864. Hot. The Rebels are tunnel hunting again. This time along the western side of the stockade I believe they only found *three*, one of them almost completed. There are men here from all regiments and from every arm of the service, Infantry, Cavalry, Artillery, Engineers, Marines, Sailors, man of war's men, niggers, sutlers, and citizens. There is one officer with us if not more, a Major of colored troops and wounded at that. He stays with his men and will stand by them to the last. Our number is diminishing by death, at the rate of 40 per day.

Saturday, May 28, 1864. Very Warm. Some of Sherman's men were brought in this afternoon captured a few miles beyond Atlanta. They could not give us much news. There is a rumor going that Charleston has fallen, but I cannot bring it within the pale of belief. I can't see where the force to take it should come from. Our ration today was beautifully small, cornbread and bacon, bacon & cornbread. Jeff Davis ought to put another letter in the title of his kingdom. "The Corn-fed-eracy" would accurately describe it. They eat nothing but corn from the highest to the lowest.

Sunday, May 29, 1864. Fair. More Prisoners arrive today, some from the Army of the Potomac and some from the Army of the Cumberland. Among the former were two of the 143d captured on the 10th near Spottsylvania. They belong to the ancient order of "K.N's" and could tell us little or nothing concerning the Regiment. It appears from official sources that the whole number of prisoners confined here is only 13,500. Not as many as I suppose but still too many for these narrow limits and destitute conditions.

Monday, May 30, 1864. Hot. After roll call took a walk around "camp" and viewed the cumulated misery of 8 months captivity, and God of Heaven what a sight it is! Wicked, cruel, and implacable as is this cursed rebellion in every aspect, its most inhuman treatment of prisoners. To look upon the suffering enclosed within these walls would move any heart not dead to human sympathies. I am glad that our friends cannot realize our condition, it would break their hearts. A few more prisoners (from Butler's Corps.) came in today. Rations reduced.

Tuesday, May 31, 1864. Hot. Not more than a dozen prisoners came in today. Don't know where they are from. This is a great place for rumors, lies and sensation reports. The "last despatch" makes Lee fall back on Richmond, Butler takes Fort Darling and he and Grant invest the City. All this is pleasant to hear but I suppose there is no more truth in it than in the other and less probable tales that daily circulate among us. Our rations today were sufficient in quantity and if the corn meal composing the vital part of them had only been sifted I would not complain. Jack bought 5 onions for three dollars.

Wednesday, June 1, 1864. Rained, a heavy shower in the afternoon. Considering the destitute condition of the camp in regard to shelter as well as everything else, such visitation can scarcely be counted as blessings. Around us as far as we can see beyond the stockade is a wilderness of pines and yet it is almost impossible to procure a couple of sticks to stretch a blanket upon as a miserable protection from sun and shower, and enough wood to cook your dinner cannot be had for less than would buy two dinners at a northern farmhouse. How long will I suffer in this cursed Confederacy.

Thursday, June 2, 1864. Warm. Heavy shower in the evening. No news from any source, more prisoners came in but they were old captives, some of them from Richmond were hostages for pirates held under threat of hanging by the United States. A rainy night produces more misery here than a famine in Ireland. There is a God-like prayer which says, curse not thine enemies, but it is very hard to keep in such a place as this. Death is relieving us by scores daily.

Friday, June 3, 1864. Rained again. More Yanks arrived, old prisoners mostly who had been left back at Danville sick and wounded. The Johnnies are tunnel hunting again, with what success I don't know. The absorbing question of Order of Exchange is much in agitation just now. Some of the new prisoners on the authority of the New York Herald, hold to the belief that an exchange will commence on the 10th of this month. For humanitys sake I hope it may be true, but I fear it is not of the fault of men.

Saturday, June 4, 1864. Rained nearly all day. The best we could do was to lay ourselves away under scanty shelter and dream of better days. I have a vivid recollection of the tedium of some rainy days at home when time like the leaden clouds overhead seemed to be at a stand still. Now if I could exchange this day for one of such, how differently I would esteem it. A day at home, rainy or otherwise, would be so many hours in Paradise compared to this miserable prison life we have here. An escaped prisoner was brought in who had got as far as Atlanta. Several escaped last night.

Sunday, June 5, 1864. Showery. The prisoners have been amusing themselves by circulating a story to the effect that the sick and wounded will be paroled tomorrow. I should like to see it but I cannot believe it till I do. If the Rebel Government were not dead to shame and every attribute of civilization they would not think of holding hundreds of poor captives, on whom Deaths signet is plainly stamped, for the poor advantage of burying them. The number of deaths last night was unusually large owing to the storm of yesterday.

Monday, June 6, 1864. Warm with showers. Our rations were issued to us raw. Considering that we have no wood to make fires and no cooking utensils, I am not very well pleased with the change. There is a low ebb in the news department since the failure of the sick & wounded Parole. I have not heard a news story today. Saw a man peddling fresh butter, price $15.00 per pound! It ought to be very strong at that price. The Rebs are making a show of having a great many men outside. I guess they fear an outbreak.

Tuesday, June 7, 1864. Rained as usual. More prisoners came in, among them [Charles] Watson of Co. "A" our Regt. He was captured on the 27th ult. while on picket about 31 miles from Richmond. He says Sergt. [Reuben] Ebert and Moses Myer and two or three more of our Co. were killed and that Charley Clendenin was wounded. According to his account the Rebels were getting well whipped but not without great loss on our side. I hope they may already see the last ditch dimly in the distance. McClellan it is said is with the Army of the Potomac.

A.J. Riddle photograph looking southeast showing the sinks along the Stockade branch of Sweetwater creek.

Wednesday, June 8, 1864. Fair. Nothing occurred to relieve the ever returning monotonous misery of this wretched place. The usual number of fights came off and in the usual style. One would think the nature of our situation would forbid such indulgences but such is not the case. Here, everyone is demoralized, tempers ordinarily good become sour and irascible, and when disputes arrive, a word and a blow are the immediate arguments brought upon it. A dozen fights a day are considered necessary to the solution of the various questions during the same time.

Thursday, June 9, 1864. Hot, Showery. Passed like many more, lying in my kennel like a dog. It would be far better for our health if we had something to do that would offer muscular exercise and I often start for a walk within our prison walls but the sickening sights and smells to be met with everywhere are harder to bear than dull activity. I wish J. Davis and Cabinet could be shut in here for a month or two and if that would not produce an exchange, I should like Old Abe and Beast Butler to take a short turn. No prisoners today and no news.

Friday, June 10, 1864. Hot. No excitement. The "Quid nuncs" are reviving rumors of exchange and parole and all this but it amounts to nothing. There is no better prospect of an exchange now then there has been for eight months past. What is the use of going to the trouble of an exchange when we are exchanging life for Death every day. By the first of October next, the Confederacy will probably hold our bodies but the immortal part of thousands of our number will be beyond its jurisdiction.

Saturday, June 11, 1864. Rumors of Parole are again raging, but I dare not believe them. About thirty received a parole at the hands of a higher power than either the U.S. or C.S. Poor worn out wretches. After life's fitful fever they sleep well. Treason has done its worse. No steel nor poison, malice domestic foreign levy, nothing can harm them further. The prayer of hundreds more must be: "Oh hasten on the waves of time, Spirit of Death. In manhood's morning youthful prime & warm thy breath."

Sunday, June 12, 1864. Rainy. Georgia climate somewhat reminds one of "Down in Lincolnshire" in respect to rainy days. Saw two fights this morning before roll call. A few prisoners from Sherman's Army came in. They bring no news. One of them says the Rebels shot an officer at Macon this morning for some minor infringement of orders. This is no new feature in their treatment of prisoners, they have shot several in this camp since we came here and have wounded one to my own knowledge.

Monday, June 13, 1864. Rainy, cold, miserable. For some reason there was no roll call this morning and this circumstance together with an order for all the sick to report to the Surgeons, for a time revived the silly idea that they were about to commence paroling us, it soon died however and will probably be resurrected in a new form tomorrow. A Macon paper says the right of Grant's Army is somewhere and the left at Bottoms Bridge, and that Sherman's plans are quite incomprehensible and therefore to be feared.

Tuesday, June 14, 1864. Cold. Rainy. A lot of prisoners escaped last night. The old Dutch Captain declined searching for them with his blood hounds alleging that enough of his dogs have been killed already. Some Yanks have dug a tunnel on this side of camp and no doubt intended to escape to-night when it unfortunately "caved" on the outside of the stockade and was thus revealed to the

Johnnies. Poor fellows they had their labor for their pains. Cucumbers offered for sale today at 1.00 apiece.

Wednesday, June 15, 1864. Cloudy, misty. Half a thousand captives were added to our number. They are from both Armies but principly from Meade's. They do not bring much news and their accounts are not very consistent. A member of the 22nd Mass. was caught in here trying to get shoemakers to take the parole of honor and make shoes for the rebels. We shaved his head, took away his papers and made him take an oath to desist from any such work in the future. Served him right. Ought to have hung him.

Thursday, June 16, 1864. Cloudy. Another instalment of prisoners arrived numbering some 700 from the Army of the Potomac. Captured about the 1st of this month. The intelligence they bring is not exciting nor very comprehensible. I have not yet learned who has been nominated for President. According to their accounts the army is from six to thirty miles from Richmond and not making much headway, but the fact is they know very little about it. Our scanty room is now completely "jammed."

Friday, June 17, 1864. Rainy. The prisoners that came in last are in a most destitute and miserable condition. The greed and hate of the rebels have scarcely left them the clothes they wore. No shelter can be had in here nor scarcely room to lie down unless in some filthy gutter. They try to allay our indignation by killing us. The stockade will be enlarged in three or four days and plenty of room will be made for us. The latest accounts say that an exchange will be made as soon as the campaign is over. God speed it, and may it be successful.

Saturday, June 18, 1864. Rained. A dry day is a very rare thing. A few more prisoners arrived convalescent from Rebel Hospitals. The latest sensation is that unnumbered transports are on the way to Savannah with rebel prisoners to exchange for us. The story is got up with so much plausibility that I am convinced the rebels connive at it if they did not invent it. They do not scruple to lie to us for the sake of keeping us in hope of speedily getting out of here. Escapes by tunneling and otherwise are of almost daily occurrence. Two left last night that have taken the parole of honor.

Sunday, June 19, 1864. Rainy. More Yanks. A man ran over the "dead line" in pursuit of a snake today when the guard on the nearest post fired at him and missed him but the charge took effect among those inside the line, seriously wounding one man in the hip and another in the head. The prisoners that came today were from Tennessee captured by Forrest's Cavalry while on a scout. They are not very well posted in regard to current events. The stockade is now so crowded as to preclude roll altogether.

Monday, June 20, 1864. Showery. Nothing new. A New York Herald brought in by one of the prisoners makes the statement that a general parole of prisoners of all classes will commence on the 7th of July and continue till the 17th. I should like to hear from better authority than the Herald but at the same time I would rather take it from a worse source than not at all. The hope of soon getting out of here however futile it may be is all that keeps us alive.

Tuesday, June 21, 1864. Showery. A very fine tunnel was revealed today almost in a state of completion. The Dutch Captain was very wrathful over it and threatened to stop the rations on the camp till it should be filled up as no attention was paid to this threat he set the niggers to work at it and destroyed it.   Another man was shot this evening down by the spring.   He inadvertently approached too near the stockade in avoiding a very muddy place in the path.   Retribution will come some day.

Wednesday, June 22, 1864.   Hot.   The daily rain of the last four weeks only amounted to a few drops.   Guess wet weather will play out.   We have no exciting intelligence from the outside world. History of a general parole of prisoners is repeated with amendments, alterations, & additions and assumes so many shapes that all semblance of truth has left it (mores the pity).   Our daily bread degenerated into mush this evening and a small allowance at that.   Grant occupies Petersburg.

Thursday, June 23, 1864.   Hot.   Received a ration of fresh Beef today.   The first I have tasted in the Confederacy.   It was raw however and we have no wood to cook it with.   It would perhaps be good for the scurvy in this condition, but not for Diarrhea.   These two diseases are carrying off great numbers of the prisoners, and sickness of all kinds is increasing.   The enlargement of the stockade they tell us will be finished in a day or two, so they said a week ago.   The excitement about an exchange has died out.   I hope it will not be revived without some foundation.

Friday, June 24, 1864.   Hot and dry.   One poor wretch died this morning within a rod of our tent, he had been suffering some time with diarrhea and scurvy.   Last night I heard him crying out calling on his mother and incoherently wandering in his speech.   When the sun had fairly risen he calmly died.   Requiescat.   Rumors of operations at Richmond and Petersburg are quite favorable.   I hope the company will soon be over.

Saturday, June 25, 1864.   Hot.   Out of wood again, out of money, out of tobacco, out of strength, out of rations and almost out of hope, so many "outs" that I would exchange all my "ins" for one more out of the cursed Confederacy.   If this d--nd conspiracy against liberty and humanity succeeded in maintaining an existence among the nations of the earth, I shall begin to lose faith in "the immutable principles of eternal justice."   Who shall ever be able to sum up the evidence against it when the world shall sit in judgement.

Sunday, June 26, 1864.   Hot.   Several new stories have been introduced today, the latest of which is that Beauregard and 15,000 men were captured at Petersburg or at Fort Darling or God knows where.   The same authority states that Ewell is on his way to capture Washington.   So it seems that we are to exchange Capitals with the rebels.   If we would only exchange prisoners with them, it would move to the purpose.   Happy day, when it comes.

Monday, June 27, 1864.   Hot.   A very many prisoners arrived today.   They confirm in some measure the reported fall of Fort Darling.   From all I can gather there has been a great deal of hard fighting around Richmond and the greatest loss of men has been on one side whether the positions gained are a sufficient compensation the sequel alone will tell.   Our rations today I am happy to record as being unusually abundant but still none to great.   Several shots were fired at prisoners but none hurt.

Tuesday, June 28, 1864.   Hot.   Rained a heavy shower in the afternoon.   No news from the outside world and I for one am becoming so indifferent and apathetic to everything that I do not desire any. I am tired of the silly lies, the senseless rumors and ambiguous facts that find their way here.   I should like to see with my own eyes the exodus of every prisoner in this den of iniquity, but I never want to hear any more lying about it.

View of the stockade on August 16th, showing "the island" between the sinks and the northern section of the camp.

Wednesday, June 29, 1864. Warm. Rained. My 27th Birth Day. Year ago today we marched from Frederick to Emmitsburg, Md. I almost wish I was marching there today. A man was killed by the gang of thieves who inhabit near the South Gate. There is an organized band of them over there who live by robbery. The Rebel authorities since the killing of this man have taken out a dozen or so of the ringleaders for punishment. They deserve death and nothing less. The man who will steal here is a wretch indeed.

Thursday, June 30, 1864. Cloudy. Considerable excitement prevails through camp today on account of ridding it of a gang of thieves, their depredations have been borne for a long time, but yesterday when they added murder to their crimes it was used to exterminate them. A police force armed with clubs has been pursuing them all day. They are taken out of the enclosure as fast as arrested. What disposition will be made of them I don't know. The ought to be hung or shot. No rations yesterday, nor none today till just night, making us fast for 30 hours.

Friday, July 1, 1864. Hot. The new stockade was opened today and all the detachments above "49" moved into it. It was worth while to move just for the sake of moving but for comforts and convenience I would much rather have stayed where we were. The distance to carry water is now considerable and the dimensions allowed us make the streets as difficult to perambulate in the new part as they were in the old. They have promised us nails and lumber and tools to build quarters, but I do not think they ever intend really to do so. Another man killed today by a prisoner.

Saturday, July 2, 1864. Hot. All quiet in all regards save one. Some Ohio Capt. has been found here within the stockade and the story goes that the officers have been all paroled and that our turn is coming so soon that he preferred waiting to going with the remainder of them and is not staying to see to the condition of his company, the larger part of which are prisoners with him. It is very silly tale and bears the lie on the very face of it. There are rumors of a fight at Marietta, but no news from either army.

Sunday, July 3, 1864. Very Warm. No rations again for what reason unknown. They made an attempt to have roll call but scarcely succeeded. A man was shot by the guard down in the old stockade tonight and they say not within a yard of the dead line. I think to use the language of fiction that is so fitting "too fine a point" on their attention, both for their sake and our own. The day may come when a settlement of accounts will be called for and the books balanced, if it ever should I am afraid they will find we are much indebted to them.

Monday, July 4, 1864. Hot, very heavy thunder showers. No excitement. A couple of prisoners from Sherman's army report fighting at Marietta but we have no reliable intelligence from any source. The cursed rebels made an excuse of reorganizing the squads for not issuing rations till just dark. One of our detachment died today from exposure and inanition. He had no shelter nor nothing to cook his rations in so he lay around anywhere till death released him.

Tuesday, July 5, 1864. Hot. Some are still such dupes as to hope that the stories about exchanging during the present month may yet turn out to be true. Day after tomorrow is the time set for the commencement.. When it comes they will have to invent a new report or put off the day. I have put it off in my mind indefinitely. I do not think our Government has made any effort to release us since the opening of this campaign nor do I think it will for some time to come. All we want is life and patience.

Wednesday, July 6, 1864. Hot. Dull. Sensations rather scarce. 315 prisoners came in from the A of P, captured on the 29th of June. They were raiders and had been 9 days within the rebel lines burning and destroying before they were captured. These with two or three batteries were unable to escape, but the main force (a Division of Cavalry) fought their way back to our lines. Very little said by the Rebs about Richmond from which I infer there is no communication at present with it.

Thursday, July 7, 1864. Hot. I was quite surprised to find an old acquaintance among the prisoners that came in yesterday. [Henry] Roberts of Co. E 3d Penn. Cavalry. He says the Regiment was not on the raid but he being detached to serve with a Battery was surrounded with it and was for the first time "gobbled up." I learn from him that Frank Williams of B Co. is dead. I hope we may live to see the Stars and Stripes waving over yankee if not rebel land but if I must stay here too long I doubt much if I will.

Friday, July 8, 1864. Very Hot. About 300 more captives arrived. They are from Sherman's Army and also from our force in South Carolina. It seems that the campaign is being presented with genuine Yankee energy and perserverance at all points. In fact the "anaconda" is about taking another turn around the Confederacy preparatory to the fatal sqeeze. It is remote that both Charleston and Atlanta are taken, no doubt this rumor is in anticipation of the fact but it goes to show that such events are not at all improbable. Rotten pork was issued for our rations today.

Saturday, July 9, 1864. Hot. Rained in the afternoon. More prisoners arrived and more are expected tomorrow. It seems that the interest & rigor that characterized the opening of the campaign has not abated a particle. The rumor that Sherman has taken Atlanta seems to gain ground. From the Army of the Potomac it is more difficult to get anything but rumors & now and then a load of prisoners. Petersburg seemed to be the theatre of events for the present and as nearly as I can learn lies between the two armies.

Sunday, July 10, 1864. Hot. Thunder showers. More prisoners arrived among them [John T.] Nealy of our Co. who was left at Lynchburg wounded. He says they had to leave Lynchburg and marched on foot to prevent being captured by our Cavalry. They marched four days the South Side R.R. having been destroyed by raiders some days previous. They had robbed him of all his clothes at the Rebel hospital and gave him an old butternut suit in return. No further report about exchanging.

Monday, July 11, 1864. On the 4th of the month a score or so of the bandits that have been preying on their fellow captives were arrested and taken out of the prison. Today six of the chief villains were brought in again under sentence of death & were hung by the neck till dead on a scaffold erected for the purpose on the south side of the stream. The day was cloudy and gloomy and seemed to darken visibly as the time (5 PM) for the execution approached. The view of the prison at that hour was one that will long remain pictured in my recollection but no language can describe it.

Tuesday, July 12, 1864. Hot. The last sensation continues in force pro tem videlicet. The hanging of the "Raiders" so called. One of them formerly belonged to Co. F 76 N.Y. from which he deserted and then came out as a substitute. The remainder of that regiment do not perhaps deserve hanging but if the character as soldiers may be apprehended from their walk and talk as prisoners they ought to be mustered out with sundry kicks to each individual member and prohibited from ever enlisting again. They are a disgrace to any service.

Wednesday, July 13, 1864. Hotter. There is a rumor circulating that a portion of the prisoners are to be directly sent to Alabama but I do not credit it. If they wish to send any I am perfectly willing to go for one, I do not suppose we would be any better off there but we are so very bad off here that I would run any risk that shows a chance. Two men were shot this morning. One of them killed down by the stream. Neither of them as I understand were the intended victim, he escaped unharmed. This generally is the case they mostly hit some innocent person.

Thursday, July 14, 1864. Hot. Some thunder but no rain. We were promised the privilege of sending out a detail for wood but the powers that be changed their mind. They took the Sergeants out and gave them another warning as they fear an attack. The old Dutch Captain threatens once more to shell the camp till there is not a man left, if any such thing is attempted. Any crowd gathering in the vicinity of the gates is to be dispersed by dropping a shell into it. Pacific measures these.

Friday, July 15, 1864. Pleasant. For some reason best known to the Confeds we were not allowed to go for wood today inconsequence where of we had no dinner and a very slim chance presents itself for supper. I found one of our Regt. today that was captured at Gettysburg more than a year ago. He is yet well and hearty though his comrades in captivity some seven or eight in number are all dead but one or two. Paul Woodburn I learn from him is dead. The mortality among us is increasing with the hot weather.

Saturday, July 16, 1864. Warm. Nothing transpired worth recording within the limited sphere of my knowledge. Someone has commenced getting names to a petition to the federal government praying for an exchange. I have not yet seen the petition itself and cannot judge of it until. I doubt not it will prove worthless for the Government must be well aware of our suffering, dying, destitute condition. Every day makes it worse. If some pestilence does not sweep us away we shall be fortunate.

Sunday, July 17, 1864. Fair and fine. Anywhere but here inside these prison walls. I could revel in pure air and Tempered sunshine of a summer sabbath, but here all days are miserable and the fairest by the effect of old association are the most unhappy. Two men were wounded near our detachment this evening by accident or design on the part of the guards. They were quietly sitting in their tent at the time at some distance from the dead line.

Monday, July 18, 1864. Cloudy. A tunnel was found in the new stockade having been revealed to the rebs by a poor miserable traitor for the paltry price of a plug of tobacco. When it was found out that he was the informer, they caught him, shaved his head branded him with the letter "T" in the forehead and beat him with many stripes and if the rebs had not took him outside I think they would have killed him tonight. He deserves hanging as well as any traitor. The prisoners are about petitioning the general and State Government for relief. No rations today.

Tuesday, July 19, 1864. Warm. Except some flying reports concerning the discomfiture of Gen. Johnston and his resignation thereupon we have no news. The Petition or memorial from the prisoners to our government has become a subject of dissension and bids fair to fall to the ground. It is in the hands of a clique who wish to do it all and take the glory to themselves (if there be any) or else have nothing to do. It is very wrong to manifest such a spirit in the prosecution of any good work but as for the petition, I don't think it will amount to anything under any circumstances.

Wednesday, July 20, 1864. Hot. There has been quite a stir among the rebs all day. Fortifications are in process of erection out at headquarters and also over at the Station. Reinforcements arrived this morning with four or five pieces of artillery. From these indications of fear on their part we are led to believe that our Cavalry are making raids through the country and if we were not so far from our lines I should hope they might pay us a visit. Kilpatrick and a few hundred gallant riders would soon scatter the force guarding us but the difficulty would be to remove us. Half a days march would tire out the strongest.

Thursday, July 21, 1864. Hot. The work of building fortifications around the Stockade goes on with renewed vigor. Prisoners brought in today captured near Atlanta disclaim all knowledge of any raiding parties from Sherman's Army. Neither is Atlanta taken yet as we have so often heard. A member of the 9th N.Y. Cavalry attempted to commit suicide this evening by cutting his throat but a dull knife frustrated his rash design. There is a prospect of dying soon enough, one and all of us without hastening our end by violence. More or less find an easy transit every day.

Friday, July 22, 1864. Hot. Dull. A few more Yankees arrived mostly from the north. Some of them were hundred day men not six weeks in the service yet and who had never seen a fight. The remainder contained the usual number of safeguards, coffeeboilers and the like, two of the latter belonging to our regiment. Of course there is no use in looking to such men for information they wouldn't know anything if they could. It seems to be a fact that Ewell or Early or some other Reb is in Maryland on a raid.

Saturday, July 23, 1864. Cloudy. Another man from our Detachment was carried to his rest this morning making the 5th or 6th since we came here. Half a dozen more will follow soon. The whole number of Deaths now must reach nearly a hundred daily. Diarrhea and Scurvy are the universal complaints, the latter is becoming quite prevalent among the prisoners captured since the opening of this campaign. This of itself speaks plainly enough the kind and quality of our rations. Better food would save hundreds of lives and shelter from sun and rain would save hundreds more. No news from any source.

Sunday, July 24, 1864. Cool for this latitude. No change in our prospects nor any rumors of change. They do say however that Hood & Sherman have fought a battle near Atlanta and the rebels claim a victory but as they invariably do this the true result remains to be known. Death is making sad work among the prisoners. I am told that 117 were carried out to the dead house today. Received rations of rice and fresh beef, with wood to cook them they would be very acceptable but we cannot eat them raw.

Monday, July 25, 1864. Warm. No new or strange transactions have come to our knowledge from the outside world. A variety of contradictory reports concerning the recent fighting at Atlanta are in circulation and they are also trying to revive the old story of exchange or parole of prisoners but those who have sense to think give no hope to any of it. The fact that the Quarter Master is employing a large force to police the camp indicates plainly enough that the rebels see no prospect of our leaving here soon. The work on the fortifications is still going on outside and tunnel hunting inside.

Union Prisoners of War at Camp Sumpter, Andersonville, Georgia.
VIEW TAKEN FROM NORTH-EAST ANGLE OF THE STOCKADE.

A photograph of the northeast section of camp, taken by A.J. Riddle, on August 16th.

Tuesday, July 26, 1864. Cloudy. Nothing new. We are becoming so used to the miseries of this place that they cease to have any effect upon us. Three men are lying dead just down our street, but they are no more objects of interest or sympathy than the living ones around them. One of them belongs to our detachment and the first fatal case of scurvy in it. A hundred and fifty men are at work covering the swamp with fresh earth from the bank on this side. They receive an extra ration for their services. It is a good work.

Wednesday, July 27, 1864. Middling. Three or four hundred prisoners arrived. "Hundred days" men from Sigels Corps, captured by Early near Martinsburg in the valley of the Shenandoah. They report an extensive raid of the rebs into Maryland with a very disastrous termination, but I find from experience that very little reliance is to placed in the stories of prisoners. Some of them say that the Commissioners of Exchange have signed the agreement for an exchange of prisoners next month. Others deny all accounts of any steps being taken in the matter whatever. To relinquish hope is like giving up life itself. So I'll hope on.

Thursday, July 28, 1864. Hot. The usual incidents of prison life occurred in the usual order rollcall, rations cooking, eating, washing and talking wore out the day. The exchange topic is being again agitated in all circles and like many other predicted events finds corroborative evidence in every trivial passing occurence. Things that otherwise would attract no attention at all are taken up and contorted to mean something because the wish being father to the thought has warped the minds of some people all out of bearing. Nothing but a good disappointment will bring them to reason.

Friday, July 29, 1864. Rained. Motion suspended. Dull misery broods over the Camp. No cheerful light is seen through any cloud--rift of the dark future, and yet there is latent hope within us, otherwise, we could not exist at all. It is the most inexplicable subject ever brought within the pale of human contemplation why men in this 19th Century and in a Christian nation should be left to suffer under such circumstances for so long a time and under such unparalleled barbarity destitution and misery. Like the Turk, I ask, "Who is Humanity."

Saturday, July 30, 1864. Hot. Except a change of Sergeants in charge of our mess I have nothing to chronicle as affecting my condition. Sergt. Patton became too neglectful of his duties and thereby lost us three days rations of wood and wood being next to vituals the dereliction was considered sufficiently great to deprive him of his office. Sergt. Sweetman of the 6 Md. was put in his place. The Rebels are again trying to get prisoners to work at shoemaking outside with what success I do not know.

Sunday, July 31, 1864. Hot. No news except the old and improbable tale that the Commissioners of Exchange for the U.S. & C.S. have met and agreed to exchange prisoners at once. There would be some semblance of truth in this if it did not assume so many different shapes and dimensions. A simple fact is not a thing ----- shapes, but a lie assumes any form and sports all the colors of the kaleidoscope. Well, God grant that the day may come when these bonds will be broken and every prisoner shall go forth from these prison walls.

Monday, August 1, 1864. Cloudy. This morning after roll call a minister of the gospel came in and preached a sermon down by the Sutlers. He also brought in a paper containing some account of the doing of the Commissioners who on the part of the two Governments are trying to effect an exchange. I did not get the sight of the paper but he (the preacher) says there is like to be an immediate and general exchange of prisoners. The difficulties heretofore in the way have been entirely removed. This is like the sight of a sail to the wave lost mariner, pleasant and hopeful but not satisfying.

Tuesday, August 2, 1864. Cloudy. Very heavy shower. The "Johnnies" are interesting themselves in our behalf today much more than usual. The sick were all ordered to report for treatment this morning and many of the most helpless cases were admitted to the hospital. It is a pity that all cannot be thus accommodated, I scarcely ever walk down to the stream for water of a morning without seeing at least one dead man lying along the road and frequently two or three of them. Another member of our regiment died yesterday (Collers of Co. G) McGlenn and Miller will hardly make a live of it unless they get better treatment than they are likely to here.

Wednesday, August 3, 1864. Hot. Some hundreds of sick men were removed out of the stockade and the great subject of conjecture has been "Where are they taken to?". Some of would-be wise ones say they are being shipped to our lines via Hilton Head but I am sorry that I cannot get sufficient evidence to support this belief. For God's sake and humanity's I hope it may be true. Stoneman's Cavalry have been raiding in the vicinity of Macon and as raiders generally do, have ended by visiting the "bull pen" here they will be apt to rest from their labors for some time if not for all time to come.

Thursday, August 4, 1864. A genuine "dog day." No sick call. No roll call. The fact that no sick were taken out today discredits the story that they are being paroled, though I have heard from "reliable authority" that the confed newspapers contain the intelligence of an exchange under the new cartel in the trans-Mississippi department. More of Stoneman's raiders came in today, they are quite destitute the Johnnies being especially severe on this class of our troops. They report Gen. Stoneman as being himself a prisoner. If they would treat officers as they do privates it would soon bring on an exchange.

Friday, August 5, 1864. Warm. Three months a prisoner and yet alive! --but feeling as though three months more would finish me. The unavoidable maltreatment of scurvy and scorbutic diseases is destroying the lives of thousands. To be kept here a twelvemonth is death. The only uncertainty is the question of time, a strong man may live his year out, or even longer, or he may not survive half that time, as six thousand graves can testify. Sights and sounds of suffering are ever present to the senses. Ye "Powers that be" I wish you could look in here but one short hour on scenes that make the angels weep.

Saturday, August 6, 1864. Very Warm. A few more prisoners added to our number from the Western Army. Tidings from Richmond and Grant's Army are not seen or heard, the fighting seems to be over unless it be with Sherman and the cavalry. Our army must be lying still around Petersburg. No sick were removed today except the usual number removed from this world to another. There is more hopeful feeling among the mess of prisoners then usual, growing out of the belief that there will soon be an exchange. But I cannot see what their hopes are granted upon, I hear nothing but lies.

Sunday, August 7, 1864. Warm. Nothing new has occured. Another murder was committed by the guard but that is nothing unusual.   The circumstances render it an unusually cool yet dastardly act and will long be remembered by those not brought up to violence and bloodshed.   The prisoner was dipping up water between the dead line and the bridge as every one does who uses water from the stream when the sentinel on the first post on the south side deliberately raised his piece and fired at him shooting him through the head and causing instant death.   He then turned around & smilingly expatiated on his exploit.

Monday, August 8, 1864. Cloudy. Rained in the afternoon. The barracks they told us they were going to build when we came into the new stockade are at last commenced. The "darks" in connection with the 27th Detachment have been carrying in lumber all day for the first edifice to be erected within these walls. The dimensions are 135 feet by 20 and this is to contain a whole detachment. This is rather a damper on those who have recently been sanguine of a general exchange, but they get over it by saying that the rebs are going to make a parole camp of this and are building the barracks for their own men. A pretty idea!

Tuesday, August 9, 1864. Very heavy rain. The stockade washed down in 5 or 6 places causing great activity among the greybacks and no small opening of eyes on the part of the yanks. If it had occurred in the night it might have been the means of some of us but as it was, no outward attempts to escape were made. We lost today's rations however by it and went hungry and wet to our nightly rest. The work of repairing the breaches and strengthening weak places occupies their whole force, niggers and all. A few more Yanks from Sherman came in but bring no interesting intelligence.

Wednesday, August 10, 1864. Pleasant. The stockade is so far repaired this morning as to admit of our receiving a beggarly ration of corn bread and raw beans or bean shells rather for the bugs had eaten out the insides of them long ago. What good raw beans will do us without a splinter of wood to cook them over is past my dull comprehension. I have often heard of starvation on Belle Island, so often that I cannot help believing it now when our own rations come down to such an inferior degree just in the heart of the most productive portion of the Confederacy. Captivity and exposure will do for us best enough without starvation.

Thursday, August 11, 1864. Another heavy rain last night made farther damages on the stockade and in consequence the negro force has been withdrawn from fortification building and set to work repairing it. They have also commenced an exterior line at some distance from this and completely surrounding it. Whether designed as an enlargement or for greater security I cannot say. The barrack building by the 27th is far enough completed to be appropriated by the destitute for a nights shelter and presents more the appearance of a lazaretto than anything else.

Friday, August 12, 1864. Hot, no rain. Rations still on the decline. An ounce or two of lean fresh beef without salt, a pint of corn meal or corn "chop" rather with a diminution measure of the detested beans are supposed to subsist us for the next twenty four hours. A few cavalry prisoners from Sherman's Army came in today. They say that Mobile has been taken and that there is heavy fighting at Atlanta. They also tell an indistinct tale about northern papers containing an order from the President to the Southern Governors to prepare to receive their prisoners now in duress. I guess they will provide for them when they get a chance.

Saturday, August 13, 1864. Cloudy. Next monday is the time set by the wiseacres for the commencement of an exchange. The conditions of which have never been agreed upon and probably never will. I find that all the talk upon this question originates right here either with the rebels or the prisoners themselves, and notwithstanding all that has been said, we are just as far from any exchange now as we were six months ago. "Whether it is nobler" to lie here and rot with scurvy or swear allegiance to the Confederacy? These are all the alternatives I can see.

Sunday, August 14, 1864. The sun shines out with a blistering scorching power and thus in one sense admonishes that it is Sunday. But no Sunday associations come with it. No casting off of worldly groveling thoughts with weekday garments, no rest from whatever weariness pursues one, no gathering to church or sabbath school, nothing to show that God's providence in providing a day of rest for erring humanity is in the least appreciated. All is one blank of misery in this wretched den on which we may sometimes write "worse" but never better. Despair darkens the already clouded firmament of hope. Death will soon be regarded as our best friend.

Monday, August 15, 1864. Hot. Dog days begin to tell on us. The heat of the sun is greater now than we have yet felt and is so unnerving to my system that I feel as weak as a child. Though in other respects my health is not particularly impaired. More than half our detachment are suffering more or less with scorbutic diseases. Some of them rotting alive with the most loathsome sores upon their feet and legs that one can imagine. The poor possibility to the latter day "exchange" faith, have not a word to say for themselves since their last prophecy failed. When will the spirit move them again?

Tuesday, August 16, 1864. Hot. More sick men were admitted to the hospital today, but more were carried out with their toes tied together than went for treatment. We are accustomed to say it is a good thing when we can get men to the hospital but in reality I suppose they are but little better off. Six were admitted from this detachment the last time and of that number four have already died. Four of our regiment have died since we came here, [William] Wilson, Miller, [Henderson] Bonham & Holland, the first belonged to our Co. The rations we now get are of the poorest kind both in quantity and quality, and sickness especially diarrhea is increasing.

Monday, August 17, 1864. Hot. Nothing new. Some rebel reinforcements went northward last night and there was great cheering and much noise over at the railroad. What it all meant no one knows & for my part no one cares. Special orders No. 11 were published this morning to the Camp. They inform each Sergeant to detail a police squad to clean the camp. They (the orders) are intended as a salve to some rebel conscience or perhaps as an offering for the soul of the Dutch Captain who it is said died last night. It is very fine to crowd men into such a place as this and then when half of them are smitten with disease and death, introduce sanitary regulations.

Thursday, August 18, 1864. Hot. No changes to record. The dull rounds of time leave us as they find us only deeper. Daily a little deeper in the mud of misery and mire of misfortune. They still issue those detestable beans to us in lieu of bread and being unable to eat them at all I find myself actually growing weak from more inanition. The work of Barrack building goes slowly on, 34 & 35 each have the frame of thin tenement up and partially roofed. Sick men from all Detachments have taken advantage of them for shelter.

Friday, August 19, 1864. Rained. Some adventurous Yank bust his bonds last night and escaped and the Rebs have been trying all the forenoon to discover his place of exit as well as the Yank himself. I hear their bloodhounds barking in the swamp so I think his chances of "clear gone" skedaddling are not very hopeful. The outer line of stockade is now almost completed so that tunneling will soon be almost an impossibility, indeed it has rarely been successful heretofore.

Saturday, August 20, 1864. Showery. A small squad of prisoners came in today. Frank Foster says that one of them told somebody and somebody told him that the 6th & 2nd Corps of the A. of P. were reinforcing Sherman in front of Atlanta. It would seem from this that the capture of Richmond is not contemplated at this stage of the game. But we have lost all interest in movements of any kind unless their consummation in some way would effect our condition. "What is Hecuba?" (Atlanta) to us or we to Hecuba.

Sunday, August 21, 1864. A rainy day. The Rebels tell us to take courage for there are hopes of exchange. Well I don't wish to accuse them of willful falsehood but it sounds very much like it to me when they talk thus. I fully believe there will be an exchange sometime, but when? Two more of our Regt. are dead. [Christian] Worth of Co. E and ----of Co. I. The last time I saw Worth he looked quite well except a little downhearted, but a man soon sinks in such a place as this. The Heartiest man in the detachment was carried out a few days since.

Monday, August 22, 1864. Cloudy. No news. Better rations than usual were received today and in greater variety consisting of corn bread, beef, pork, corn meal and beans. Simmer with his gangrene foot was taken out to hospital this morning. It seems that most if not all of those who proceeded him from this detachment are now dead. Father Abraham I wish you had my ration of wood to boil coffee with for your family. I think you would soon bring on an exchange. I further think you had much better do it anyhow.

Tuesday, August 23, 1864. Hot. Three months today since we entered this abode of wretchedness. In those three months one eighth of the original number have been "exchanged." And another eighth have sure passports over Jordan by the next train. Ye, people of the North do ye know this? Do you know that 30,000 men, fathers, sons, brothers, and kindred are rotting, dying by inches in the most loathsome captivity, and for what? If ye know speak and tell us, if not, ask your rulers and demand an answer. It is time our cause should be heard.

Wednesday, August 24, 1864. Hot. The only unusual occurrence within the sphere of my knowledge today was a case of suicide in the next Detachment. Robert Sheilds of the 76th N.Y. having a greater dread of this life more than the King of terror, tied his suspenders to his "rooftree" in the form of a noose and deliberately choked out the vital spark by strangulation or suffocation or whatever the proper word may be for such dishonorable exit.

"When all the blandishments of life are gone, the coward shrinks to death, the brave live on." There is greater provocation for such deeds here than in many circumstances in life, but the complete above expresses my ideas on the subject of suicide.

Thursday, August 25, 1864. Hot. Nothing new. No signs of ever getting out of this miserable slave pen. Some half dozen officers of negro troops were taken out as well as two or three sergts. who labor under the imputation of holding commissions. The supposition arriving from this fact is that the officers are being exchanged but there are many other solutions more plausible. Ellis, the gambler sutler and general swindler has vacated the camp having made enough money I suppose to buy his way out. Such men are only loyal to their own interest.

Friday, August 26, 1864. Very hot. One would think summer is just coming on instead of going off, comparing the present heats with those of the last month. The moskitoes too just beginning to make night hideous with their patience tiring note of combat, curse them, how they have bit me these last two evenings. The Q.M. has changed the programme in his dept. and now gives us cooked rations (so called) instead of raw. We are not the any way thankful for the change as the quantity is only smaller and the quality more inferior then when served in the natural state.

UNION PRISONERS OF WAR AT CAMP SUMPTER, ANDERSONVILLE, GA
NORTH-EAST VIEW—TAKEN FROM THE STOCKADE.

Photograph taken by A. J. Riddle on August 16, 1864.

Saturday, August 27, 1864. Warm. Some of the clothing sent by the U.S. government to the Richmond prisoners found its way here yesterday. This circumstance is of little account one way or another, but like anything else the over credulous seize upon it. Every one says the exchange of prisoners is near at hand and cite this tale and that as evidence to convince nobody that he (nobody) is quite behind the times with his unbelief, but in spite of all, nobody thus far has much the best of it.

Sunday, August 28, 1864. A thunder shower last night cleared the air for a lovely day. The sky is as pure and cloudless as the heaven it emblems. Such sabbath days as these remind me of home and old times so strongly as to almost make me feel heartsick and homesick. A few prisoners from Atlanta arrived, they report Sherman as still working at the rebels but not as though he arrived at Atlanta. The Rebel Sergeant that counts our Detachment says their papers state that, the exchange agents cannot agree and that there will be no exchange or parole during the war.

Monday, August 29, 1864. Cloudy. I am sick today in body and soul. Physically with diarrhea, mentally with discontent and despair. The unnumbered lies that have been told us concerning an exchange of prisoners has worn out my patience, while exposure and bad diet has almost worn out my body. Up to 4 o'clock this afternoon one hundred and twenty-five deaths had been recorded at the hospital as the quota for this day. What do you think of that Father Abraham? Could you enlist that many in a day? I have a good mind to curse all governments, Federal, confederate, and every other kind.

Tuesday, August 30, 1864. Warm. Still unwell. The summer is plenty on the decline the days seem to be as hot as ever but the nights are getting colder. Whether a change of season will be better or worse for us remains to be seen. The mortality just now has never been as great heretofore and is more likely to increase than diminish. God of Heaven what a thing it is for men to suffer and die as they do here. When in the world's history can you find another such Golgotha as this? The "black hole" was a mere drop in the ocean compared with it. We offer more sacrifices every day.

Wednesday, August 31, 1864. Hot. Another month has almost passed and yet we live and suffer. How many more will pass us in the same condition? Is there no hope, no prospect of ever living again in a better land and like human beings? Little I am afraid. I hope that we in our ignorance are mistaken when we think, and speak bitterly against our government for its seeming heartlessness toward us. It may be that circumstances justify the keeping us here.

Thursday, Sept. 1, 1864. Warm and clear with a fine blue sky. There is much talk in camp today about the rebel proposition to exchange and the probability of its being accepted by our Government. Some are quite confident that it will be, but when we consider that it leaves Lincoln's pets, the confiscated contrabands, out in the cold we can easily judge what reception it will meet with at Washington. Our Detachments will soon be one grand corps of cripples with the scurvy. I think I am getting it myself.

Friday, Sept. 2, 1864. Warm. Something wrong again this morning. Somebody missing (torn to pieces by the bloodhounds I believe) and no rations to be issued till the rebs find out who he is and where he belongs. The excitement of discussing the exchange question is running down. Some say that the proposition to exchange as agreed upon by the commissioners has been rejected by the

Federal government, if this is really the case good-bye to hope, and may Old Abe and his Cabinet sink in a deeper hole than that which opened under the Forum.

Saturday, Sept. 3, 1864.   Cloudy.   The last report now epidemic is that Sherman has given Hood a bitter dose of Yankee tactics that he has flanked Atlanta and left it with a whole corps of Rebs almost in his rear yet without endangering his position.   It is also rumored that Grant and Lee have been maneuvering with some fighting on McClellan's old battle ground before Richmond.   Whatever may have been the result the rebels do not consider it worthy of rejoicing.   Fight on ye heroes, fight us out of here if you can.

Sunday, Sept. 4, 1864.   Cloudy.   Dullness and leaden-hard misery prevails.   The hopes of exchange during the present month has bloomed and faded and produced no fruit except a few bitter kernels of disappointment.   It appears that the federal government thinks more of a few hundred niggers than of the thirty thousand white here in bondage.   He may be right in his views (Father Abraham I mean) of the question, but I cannot think so, neither expedience nor humanity demand or justify our suffering.

Monday, Sept. 5, 1864.   Fair & Warm.   The Rebel guards murdered another man for us last night a member of the 7th Ind.   He was lying in his tent asleep and one of his messmates was moving outside near but not over the "dead line."   The guard fired at the one outside and missed him but killed the unconscious sleeper within.   He was shot through the superior portion of the skull and the brain scattered all about.   The latest news confirms the defeat of Hood's Army near Jonesboro and the victorious advance of Sherman.

Tuesday, Sept. 6, 1864.   Rained.   The Camp is wild with excitement this evening consequent upon an order for the first eighteen detachments to be ready to leave tomorrow or may be tonight. Some are confident that we are going to be exchanged others look at it a change of prisons only.   I shall be better satisfied with the latter than with no change at all, but God grant that it may be something better that it may be the commencement of the good time coming.   Whatever the end may be it has cheered up many a desponding heart for the time being.

Wednesday, Sept. 7, 1864.   Hot.   Thank God I have lived to see a day of rejoicing for at least a portion of the miserable wretches whom I call my fellow prisoners.   Ten Detachments have gone out of the stockade and are being shipped on board the cars.   The rebs assure us that there is an exchange and that they are not moving us for the sake of greater safety.   They further assure us that every prisoner will be out of here by the 20th of the month.   This I rather doubt but I am willing to stay six weeks longer if I can only be sure of my chance then.   One of our Mess died last night, [J] Connell [14th U.S.] by name.

Thursday, Sept. 8, 1864.   Cloudy.   More prisoners left today and during the night it is expected some ten detachments will get "marching orders."   There is much anxiety to know where we are going. We all hope and most of us believe there is an exchange going on but some are so desponding and incredulous that they cannot see anything but a change of prisons.   I hope I shall have occasion to demonstrate their error by my own experience.

Friday, Sept. 9, 1864.   Warm.   A few more captives were sent off.   The Rebs seem to be hurrying us along as fast as they can but their roads and rolling stock is in such condition that they make but slow progress. The detachment from 1 up to 18 have gone from this side of the stream and some of the higher numbers from the other side. The sick and cripples are left behind and for the present occupy the barracks and hospital. Several of our mess "flanked out" last night. Putnam died this afternoon.

Saturday, Sept. 10, 1864. Warm. "The cry is still the go." God speed the good work if they are going as we believe out of the Confederacy, and may our turn come soon. I feel that to stay here much longer, will be to stay forever not only for me but for hundreds. Men are dying here faster than ever and the number of cripples is quite astonishing. Half that remain of our detachment are scarcely able to walk from scurvy and gangrene sores.

Sunday, Sept. 11, 1864. Warm. Our detachment received marching orders about 4 PM and we immediately packed up the few articles belonging to us and fell in line over at the south gate to wait for the train that shall take us but as there are seven detachments ahead of ours I do not think we will get off with the first load. The belief that we are going to be exchanged is giving way to a more unpleasant apprehension. It looks now more like a "military necessity" than any thing else. Hood falling back leaves us on Sherman's flank.

Monday, Sept. 12, 1864. Hot. Four Detachments left this morning. We lay in the sun among the fleas till near dark and then left also. My emotions at passing out the gate were not what they would have been if I had been sure of a speedy transit to the federal lines. Nevertheless I am glad to escape the horrors of this place for a time even though others as bad await us in some other portion of the Confederacy. They have given us three days rations of cornbread & bacon, and we are moving, but our destination is unknown.

Thursday, Sept. 15, 1864. Hot. Reached Florence S.C. at daylight, 64 miles from Kingsville, weary, worn out and sick both in body and spirit. We do not seem to be destined for any farther point at present as the train load that left before us at Anderson met us here via Charleston. We have been kept on board the cars all day, till now (sundown). We are now camped in the field about a mile from the Station. We were loaded up about 12 M to come out here but the car I was in ran off the track and caused a long delay. No rations have been received today although we are entirely out.

Friday, Sept. 16, 1864. Last night was very chilly but this is one of the hottest days I have ever seen. A Ration of cornmeal was received this morning about daylight, the first we have drawn since last monday night. They say (and it is very easy to believe) that they had no time to give them, to prepare a place for us, or provide substance beforehand. The meal we received was hot from the mill and very palatable when cooked. Our guards are very fond of trading and treat us quite kindly, not like the Georgians.

Saturday, Sept. 17, 1864. Hot. Our new situation is becoming more endurable. Rations of rice and bacon, corn meal and salt have been received to day and hungry yanks have done them ample justice. We are allowed greater liberty here than in any place we have been yet. Trading and talking with the guard is freely permitted, and rings, knives, jackets, boots, shoes, and clothing of all kinds is bartered for sweet potatoes, grapes, apples etc. etc. The guard is composed of boys and old men and illustrates one case where "extremes meet".

Sunday, Sept. 18, 1864. Cloudy. We are beginning to think ourselves fortunate in being sent to Florence S.C. for safer keeping than Camp Sumter afforded. We receive good rations with the promise of even better, and notwithstanding the large number that have tried to escape, they allow us the largest liberty consistent with our condition as captives.   They seem to have some sympathy for our sufferings and would alleviate them if it lay in their power.   Sold my vest for fifteen confederate dollars.

Monday, Sept. 19, 1864.   Cloudy.   We only received a ration of beans and pork today.   Fodder is pretty scarce in this region and I am afraid we will suffer for it.   Sweet potatoes seem to be plenty but they prefer selling or trading them to issuing them to us.   Numbers of yanks were brought in who had ran away, they say that the country is alive with militia and that escape "to the happy land of Caanan" is quite impossible.   They generally come back well laden with forage and I suppose that makes amends for the greatest failure.   Harris has not been returned yet.

Tuesday, Sept. 20, 1864.   Cloudy.   Nothing new.   Corn meal seems to have "played out" nothing to eat today but rice and beans and not enough of that.   I am pretty sure we would get enough here if they had it to give us but the commissary is empty.   Trading across the lines has been stopped so that it is rather difficult to come by anything now except what they issue to us. Water is still our greatest want, there being but one well in the camp and the stream is so far off that not many squads can be conducted to & from it.

Wednesday, Sept. 21, 1864.   Cloudy.   Short of rations.   Apples of the poorest quality are sold at $20 per bushel Confederate money, and sweet potatoes at about the same rate.   This is a great falling off from Camp Sumter prices where the same rates prevailed in U.S. Money, but it is still a starvation tariff.   They have at last furnished shovels for the purpose of digging wells hope we will soon obtain a supply of the great purifier.   Wrote an application to the commanding officer of the post for employment upon the records of the camp, guess it will not be successful.

Thursday, Sept. 22, 1864.   Rained.   Monotonous.   We have become domiciled in our new home and pursue our courses of thought and action just about as we used to.   There does not seem to be a very deep feeling of disappointment among us that our journey ends so far short of the summit of our hope, but this may be accounted for by the fact that the conviction that we were going to be exchanged was not deeply rooted, though circumstances conspired to give it that effect.

Friday, Sept. 23, 1864.   Rained heavily.   Flooding the greater portion of the camp and making housless prisoners damply miserable.   There are not so many destitute ones here as at Camp Sumter but still enough to excite compassion in any breast not dead to human feelings.   Rations today were minus meat of any kind and still reduced in quantity.   The Rebs complain a good deal of the scarcity of "grub" and consequent difficulty of supplying us, and I suppose we must believe them when they say they are doing the best they can.

Saturday, Sept. 24, 1864.   Rained.   The weather seems to be in a fickle mood probably on account of old Sols deserting the northern hemisphere or according to astronomical tradition "crossing the line."   Our Q.M. has scared up some of Pharoahs "lean kin" or some other ghostly herd of bovines and given us a ration of animal fibre as destitute of fat as his soul is of grace, in other words as greaseless as he is graceless.   Southern Confederacy you are a miserable failure and I wish you would let me pass out.

Sunday, Sept. 25, 1864. Clear and fine. The sabbath has been kept with fasting by the greater portion of the camp as no rations have been issued today but not with prayer, anathemas against the Confederacy, Jeff Davis, Abe Lincoln and other potentates are all the invocations that have gone up from this vicinity from the rising to the setting of the sun. For news we have a story that Hood & Sherman have been exchanging prisoners and that Grant has defeated Lee at Winchester. How much truth there is in it all I know not.

Monday, Sept. 26, 1864. Splendid weather. Too fine to pass in such a place as this without exciting old recollections of such glorious autumn spent in a happier land. To think of them makes me homesick. What would I not give to be at home tonight, even if I had to return to my captivity tomorrow. As yet I dare not hope on the probability of release. We seem to be cut off and forgotten both by our friends and enemies left to linger on, to suffer, to die and sink in oblivion under the great ocean of existence. Well, let us endure while we can.

Tuesday, Sept. 27, 1864. Fair. Nothing notable to mark against this day. The Camp is raving with hunger and talking all kinds rash and unreasonable things in consequence, but this is almost an everyday affair. If we do not ultimately starve to death I shall be thankful. The rebels continue to tell us that they will give us more by and by, but I think they are lying wilfully to keep the men quiet. Whatever may be the reason the chances of growing fat on Confederate "grub" are daily diminishing. We receive less than half rations.

Wednesday, Sept. 28, 1864. Fair. The Rebs have been taking the names of those among us who are willing to swear fealty to the Confederacy and find plenty in that condition. Some driven to it by starvation and despair, others by their own inherent worthlessness and still others by the hope of being thus enabled to reach our own lines then to abjure their new faith and take up the old. In any case I consider it very disreputable and entirely unbecoming a soldier of the United States. I am not yet tired of my allegiance to the stars and stripes--long may they wave.

Thursday, Sept. 29, 1864. Warm. The promised increase of rations has not yet come to be a thing of fact, in my opinion it never will. Sweet Potatoes were issued to us today at the astonishing rate of one bushel to 275 men or about one third of a small potato to each man. Shades of Hooker! what a ration! Read Ben Butler's letter of the 4th of August to the rebel commissioner of exchange, it is a pretty document, worthy of its author, and vindicates the United States from the aspersions of neglect that I have so often heard cast upon it.

Friday, Sept. 30, 1864. Hot. Starvation still prevails and is like to. Confederate supplies are running low. How under the heaven we are to live on this grub is a question for the philosophers and physiologists to decide. I give it up as being beyond the range of my analytical powers. They now turn upon us when we complain and accuse us of starving their prisoners to death. A baser lie than this was never coined ever in their own lying confederacy and meets with that contempt and derision it merits. We *ought* to starve them in retaliation.

Saturday, October 1, 1864. [In pencil] Warm. My ink has failed me and I have sold my gold pen, so these durned scribbling must necessarily come to an end.

Sunday, October 2, 1864. Moved into the stockade. The general aspect of the place so resembles Camp Sumter that we will soon forget that it is not the same place. There is the same swamp, the same dirty stream and in course of time will be the same filth, sickness and misery that characterize that den of wretchedness.   The prisoners from Charleston are being transported here as fast as circumstances will allow.   Rations very slim.

Monday, October 10, 1864.   Cold & clear.   Frost last night causing much suffering among the destitute.   Slept very cold myself.   What will we do when winter comes?

Tuesday, October 11, 1864.   Frost again last night.   A new Officer from Charleston has taken command of the camp & promises to perform well.   We have already received better rations and he is going to protect us from the extortions of petty trading by regulating the price of all articles sold in camp.

[Written March 15, 1865.]   The promises of the new Commander failed.   He turned out to be a Confederate instead of the gentleman we took him for.

Friday, November 4, 1864.   Sick and miserable.   Got a very bad cold and symptoms of inflammatory rheumatism.   I have never known what misery is till within the last two weeks, during that time I have not been warm for a single moment unless when asleep.   This constant chill has nearly upset me and unless it leaves me soon will be the death of me.   My condition would be bad enough if I had the best of companions to share it, but my tent mates are only an additional aggravation.   They cannot rise above the lowest level of humanity.   What in Heaven's name were some men made for?   A man whose mind can comprehend nothing beyond the relative values of "confed" and "greenbacks" whose whole soul can be covered with a ten cent postage currency, who can talk of nothing but paltry trading and whose time is spent in wringing five cent pieces from poverty stricken fellow mortals constitutes an anomaly that should not exist.   Nevertheless it does, and it is my misfortune to be intimately associated with it.   I hope the day may come that will release me from all such grievances and allow me to choose my own company.   It cannot be that the war will last forever or that we must always suffer in captivity.   Well, God's will be done.

Wednesday, Nov. 9, 1864.   Cold & cloudy.   Encouraged by the Rebs (who by the way are all McClellan men) the prisoners, held an election for president of the United States.   The ballots used were beans, red for McClellan and white for Old Abe.   Two McClellan and one Lincoln man presided at the polls.   The voting commenced and continued till Old Abe's bean bag contained nearly a quart while that of his opponent could boast but a meagre handful.   Then the McClellan men broke up the election and left in disgust.

Saturday, November 26, 1864.   Pleasant.   The last few days and nights have been extremely cold and we have suffered accordingly, quite a number having perished from the cold.   Our rations have also been reduced to a pint of meal or rice per day.   They say the cause of this reduction is Sherman's recent movements in Georgia, cutting off their supplies in that region.   We shall inevitably starve on such an allowance.   A batch of letters came last night, but none for me.

Sunday, November 27, 1864.   The day of Jubilee is at hand and those for whom it came are accordingly jubilant.   The inmates of the hospital are undergoing the process of paroling and some 1000 or 1500 will leave here tomorrow for Yankeeland.   Ten thousand is to be the limit of this exchange and is to include only sick and convalescent.

Sunday, December 25, 1864. Cold. The Rebels for a Christmas diversion drove us across the creek and counted us back again as they are in the habit of doing. My Christmas dinner today would not do much honor to the table of an epicure but was still quite a feast for a prisoner consisting of beans and sweet potatoes boiled together and a generous quantity of cornbread manufactured by myself, especially for this occasion. Meat we have not seen for more than forty days.

Monday, December 26, 1864. Rainy. No comfort to be found either in retrospection, anticipation or the contemplation of the present. The gnawing of appetite assail us more than half of the time and cold and wet the remainder. No prospect of any further exchange nor any hopes of better rations. Curse your Confederacy. I wish I was well out of it.

This is the final entry for Keys' diary. Sgt. Keys was paroled on February 27, 1865, at N.E. Ferry, N.C., and later was mustered out with his company on June 12, 1865. He died on August 21, 1917.

PRISONERS RECEIVING RATIONS.

Robert Holmes, (left) Musician, Co. B, 16th Connecticut Infantry was captured on April 20, 1864 at Plymouth, N.C., and sent to Andersonville. He was paroled at Charleston, S.C., on December 11, 1864. Private Jasper N. Finney, (right) Co. E, 4th Indiana Cavalry, was captured on July 20, 1864 near Newnan, Ga. He eventually escaped and returned to his regiment on September 23, 1864 near Carterville, Ga.

Part Five
"That darkest of all hours."

Memoirs of John Simmons, William W. Jellison, Eli J. Wamsley, Ichabod Preston

JOHN SIMMONS alias JOHN HALL
Company C, 49th New York Infantry, Sixth Corps.
Age: 20.
Enlisted on Sept. 20, 1861.
Captured at Spotsylvania Court House, May 12, 1864.

Before we entered the stockade we were searched, and anything that could be found upon us of value was taken from us--money, clothes, shoes, knives, and the like. In some instances, money, watches, etc., were passed slyly down the line, to another prisoner, and perhaps recovered by the owner after he had been through the searching ordeal and had gotten inside the stockade.

My Sergeant was John Freelove, of the 2d Vt., and it was his duty to draw rations, for which he received two rations for himself. About every two weeks, or longer, we might get a piece of bacon or beef, about half the length of two fingers and about as wide and thick. If we got a small bone in our meat, soup was made with it, keeping it until the next day, then crack it and cook it again with our corn meal, making a mighty weak kind of soup, without salt. Once in two weeks a half pint of small white beans was given us. The filthiness and repulsiveness of what I saw men eat is not to be uttered or written for civilized ears and eyes. Men, because of craving of hunger, ate anything they could get. They would beg and cry, night and day, for more to eat, and many a poor fellow became crazy from hunger and exposure. One day when the gate was open, as the wagon passed out with dead bodies, a black dog ran in, and in a moment a hundred men were after him, and those who could not rise from the ground struck at him as he passed. He lived only a few moments. He was literally torn in shreds, and some did not wait to cook his flesh, but ate it raw. Every bone was eagerly sought by starving men. My own hunger at this time I can not describe. The sights I beheld no one would believe, unless they had seen them for themselves. Men would tear the hair from their heads and howl like madmen, as many of them were, and fall to the ground, never to rise again. Many there were whom it was dangerous to be near, for fear of being injured or bitten by them.

Water becoming very scarce, wells or holes were dug, the men using anything they could find that would throw up dirt. A little water was now and then obtained in this way, its quality but little better than that which came from the stream. Some holes that were dug served another purpose, especially those as near the dead line as we dared to dig. At night from the holes a trench was dug toward the stockade for the purpose of tunnelling out. I assisted in one of these, and we had gotten beyond the stockade, when one of our fellow-prisoners informed the rebel Quartermaster. His compensation was a plug of tobacco. The informer lost his tobacco and was made to run the gantlet, while each fellow-prisoner gave him a kick. He received such usage that he nearly died. He was removed by the rebel Quartermaster, and we never saw him again.

The first sight to a new prisoner as he came into the pen caused him at once to be thoroughly disheartened, and I saw many soon after they came in, sit down, and it seemed to me they never rose up again, but sat there moaning and crying until they died; and then they were carried out and thrown in the trench, never to be heard of again by us or by their friends at home.

WILLIAM W. JELLISON

Company E., 96th Illinois Infantry, Fourth Corps.
Age: 31.

I was captured at Atlanta about the 20th of August, 1864; was taken to Andersonville with a number of Stoneman's raiders; was robbed of coat, hat, and all the little treasures I had on my person; was told by my captors that I would have good quarters in the prison. One man took my rubber coat, another traded hats with me and gave me one of much less value. Soon another came and traded also. They kept on trading until I was hatless and coatless, and in this situation was turned into that slaughter-pen at Andersonville. It would be useless for me to attempt to describe my feelings as I entered the gate of that prison and looked upon the ghastly corpses of some seventy-five prisoners, naked as when they were born, bloated and dirty, many of them covered with filth; eyes staring wide open, and limbs drawn up. This was my first introduction,--this was the first sight that met my gaze. I firmly believe, and shall till my dying day, that my hair rose on end and the blood curdled in my veins as I beheld that sight. There crowded around me living skeletons, with sunken eyes and long matted, tangled hair, dirty and filthy, many of them with not enough clothing to cover their nakedness. I find that language is too weak to picture the horrid scene. Had I the tongue of an angel I could not do it. None can understand what I write--only those who witnessed the same. Those Southern prison hells are in one respect like religion. To understand it, you must have an experience. Every survivor of Andersonville that was there in the fall of '64 will know whether I am writing truth or fiction. As those sickly, starved, and grimy looking beings crowded around me, so eager to hear the news from the army, I looked upon them and grew sick at heart. That scene will haunt me while I live. For a little while only I gave up in despair, and made up my mind that I, too, would soon be as one of them. I believe that if ever I offered an earnest prayer it was at that darkest of all dark hours.

I prayed fervently for grace to sustain me, for I saw no ray of hope or spark of light from the dreary scene around, and, like one of old, I can truthfully say God heard and answered my prayer. Had I at that time given way to that awful feeling of despondency that was creeping over me, like many others I would have been carried out and my dust be mingled with that of thousands of others in South Georgia.

I was turned into the prison about four p.m., as near as I can recollect, the 24th of August, 1864, and was placed in a detachment. I then had time to think and look around, and wonder where the good quarters were that my captors told me I would have;--so good and comfortable that I would not need coat or hat. While I was looking and wondering, my name was spoken, and looking behind me I saw one of my company boys (Charley Heath), who was captured at Chickamauga. He invited me home with him. I asked him where he lived, and he led the way to his abode, which was a hole in the ground. I remained with him as long as prison life lasted. It seemed they had just drawn their rations. As he was ready to dine, he asked me if I would share his hospitality. His bill of fare consisted of corn-meal gruel, quite thin and saltless. I tasted thereof, and came near heaving Jonah. He remarked that I would come to it before long.

After we had conversed together in the darkness and gloom of that prison until the sentinels had

Giving up the Ghost

called out "ten o'clock and all is well," Heath said: "I guess we had better retire," and we both crawled into the hole which he called his home. Then commenced the bodily torture of being eaten up alive. I had been a soldier for over two years and a half, and thought I knew something about graybacks, but my pen fails me when I attempt to describe how they tortured me that night and all the following nights of my prison life. The whole pen was literally alive with crawling vermin. I lay about thirty minutes, but could stand it no longer; got up and attempted to walk around, but the darkness was so intense that I could not see where I was going; so I had just to stand and stamp and shake myself for hours, and each hour seemed an age. I thought morning would never come. That night seemed longer than the two and a half years of active soldier life on the battle-field. All through those hours of intense suffering I thought of home and loved ones, of wife and sweet babies, wondering if I should ever see them again. Morning came at last. Weary and exhausted with the sufferings of the past night, in which I had not slept one wink, I began to look around me, and the horrors that met my gaze that day will haunt me while I live.

EXECUTION OF UNION PRISONERS.

PRIVATE ELI J. WAMSLEY
Company E, 65th Indiana Infantry, Twenty-third Corps.
Age: 36.
Captured in East Tennessee, Dec. 16, 1863.
Entered Andersonville on March 14, 1864.

On the 11th of July, when the six raiders were hanged, Captain Wirz had a gallows erected inside the stockade for the purpose, and the time was set for the execution, and the prisoners marched in. When they saw the awful reality before them, one of them made a desperate effort to get away, which caused a general stampede among the prisoners, and in the rush I was shoved head foremost into one of those wells about thirty feet deep, my left shoulder being dislocated in the fall. I remained in the well until the men were hanged, and then the ropes were used in getting me out of the well. I owe my deliverance from that living grave chiefly to a member of the Fourteenth Illinois cavalry. I believe his name was Noah. His surname I cannot recollect, but he has the gratitude of my heart all the same.

Eli Wamsley was paroled on December 10, 1864 in Wilmington, N.C.

INTERIOR VIEW OF THE HOSPITAL.

PRIVATE ICHABOD PRESTON
Company D, 85th New York Infantry, Fourth Corps.
Age: 25.
Captured at Plymouth, N.C. on April 20, 1864
Entered Andersonville on May 1, 1864.

Early in June, 1864, I was taken sick with typhoid fever and removed to the hospital, where I remained about three months, and made a narrow escape from death. When I became convalescent I was detailed as assistant hospital steward, and served quite a long time. I was then assigned to the duty of getting out the medicine at the drugstore, and was provided with a pass which permitted me to leave the stockade at any time during the day. I was in habit of going over to the depot, and in that event to visit three boys of Company H, of my regiment. They were on a detail in the commissary department. While visiting them one day, I slipped over and gave a piece of poisoned sponge to a bloodhound. I did not dare to mention the fact to anybody while I was at Andersonville; for one could hardly trust his best friend there. I heard a rebel sergeant say the next day that it was a d----d Yankee that had done it, and that he would give $100 to find out who it was. The sergeant's name was Smith--Crooked Neck Smith, we used to call him. I wonder if he would give as much now? It was my intention to give the rest of the dogs a similar dose, but was afraid of being caught. Detection would have meant death to me, beyond a doubt. But for those dogs I would not have staid in that prison hell as long as a whole year, as I did. I always believed I could out-general the rebs but for the dogs.

Part Six

"Death is doing his share of the work faithfully."

Diary of George Hitchcock

PRIVATE GEORGE A. HITCHCOCK
Age: 20
Company A, 21st Massachusetts Infantry, Ninth Army Corps.
Captured in the battle of Bethesda Church, June 2, 1864.
Confined at Andersonville, Millen, and Florence prisons.

Thursday, June 16th. Reached the gates of the Andersonville stockade soon after noon, where we were taken in charge by Captain Wirz, a grizzly, dirty-looking Dutchman. As we stand on the outside of the stockade, on the rising slope near the headquarters of Captain Wirz, waiting for our names to be enrolled, our eyes take in a view of the inside of the "hell upon earth" we are about to enter. We saw a dense, black mass of seething, moving humanity, not unlike the appearance of a mammoth ant-hill just broken open, covering the whole space enclosed, except a swampy valley in the centre, through which flowed a sluggish stream. Over the whole hung a cloud of black smoke from thousands of little fires, where rations were being cooked. As soon as the enrollment is completed, we pass through the heavy-timbered double gate, and are shut out from the world.

As we pass along through the dense crowd of fellow-prisoners who are looking for familiar faces, we see squalor and filth everywhere. The pitch-pine smoke has given even the clearest complexion an Afric hue, and we are assured that this will be our own fate in a week or two. As we move along we find that the crowd which pressed against us near the gates does not decrease. Anxious to secure a good clear spot where we may sit down, I break away from our crowd, but do not find my desired haven. I am told that I had better sit down where I can find a chance, for if I wait until dark I may not find even room to stretch out. I accept the advice and "squat," while Jim Miller goes to hunt up the 21st boys who were lost at the Wilderness and Spottsylvania. The first familiar face I saw was [Ransom] Bailey, of Company I, and at last the mystery of his fate was solved. He had been missing since the 23rd of last December, when on our widely-deployed skirmished line, advancing through tangled underbrush and dense thickets near Blain's Cross Roads, East Tennessee; while passing through one of these thickets, Bailey, my right guide, was missing, and not seen again.

**New arrivals at Andersonville were often greeted
with the jeer, "Fresh fish!".**

He tells a story of hardship which makes the heart ache. Being swooped up by two guerrillas in the dense thicket, he was hurried forward on a lonely path over mountains, and, evading our outposts, was made to march ninety miles to Bristol, from thence to Richmond, where he was confined at Belle Isle through the winter, and early in the spring was brought down here. He is troubled with scurvy, and complains of the cold nights, for he has worn out all his clothing; a pair of ragged cotton drawers compose his only covering. His face, black as a negro's, is hardly recognizable. He directed us to the spot where we found Sergeant [J. Albert] Osgood, [Wilber A.] Potter, and ten others of the 21st. A sorry looking set of fellows, poor and emaciated, though prisoners only six weeks. The day was passed in hearing the accounts of the horrors which seem to be our inevitable lot. We returned to our squatting place, James Miller and myself, sadly out of spirits, each of us hoping that our friends will never hear how we are situated. As we lie down on our bed of clay, we are cautioned to "freeze" to our ration bags; so we fasten them to our blouses and essay to sleep. At ten o'clock, however, we awake from a doze and find the rain falling. We sit up till morning drenched to the skin. Thus ends our first day at Andersonville.

June 17th. We found three men from Sherman's army, who have just come in, and one has a woolen blanket. We have gone in together, and, after looking several hours, secure sticks, and set up a shelter. Five of us get under, but find that we can only lie on our backs. There are now over 20,000 prisoners here, and the stench in every part of the camp is well-nigh unendurable. We are assured, however, that we shall get accustomed to that after a few days. Great numbers are dying every day, many from scurvy. At night drew rations of rice and sow-belly; the rice is half-cooked, and only half a pint of it at that.

June 18th. Our squad was called to the gate and divided. As several of our number could not be found, the Dutchman informed us that we would not have any rations until the missing men were produced. It seemed like hunting for a needle in a hay-mow, but our stomachs craved, and each man made an energetic search until all were found.

We are formed into the eighty-third detachment (of 270 men each). Each detachment is divided into three squads, of 90 men each. Rebel sergeants call the roll of the detachments every morning. A Union sergeant is assigned to each squad, and, when the ration wagons come in, goes with a detail from the squad and gets and distributes their rations. These are the only camp regulations. The rations are brought into camp in the latter part of the afternoon. The view of the country outside is a dreary monotony of pine forest, circling around us half a mile away. The centre of the camp is an impassable swamp, where all refuse matter of 25,000 men is thrown and deposited. It has become a mass of corruption, living with worms, and would alone be reason enough for the dreadful mortality which increases every day. Several prisoners for [Maj-Gen. Franz] Sigel's West Virginia Army came in to-day, many of them wounded, whose wounds have not yet been dressed. Thirty-six prisoners, while out under guard getting wood, escaped by overpowering the guard, driving them along with them. Our rations to-day were corn-bread, two inches square, and sow-belly.

June 19th. Very hot. Heavy shower in the afternoon. A lot of prisoners from Sherman's and Butler's army came in. [James A.] Miller and [Thomas B.] Dyer sick with the diarrhea. Found Walter Lamb, of the 25th Massachusetts, who was taken prisoner June 3rd at Cold Harbor. Two men were shot by a sentry who fired at another prisoner, who had gotten over the "dead-line," a little rail running around the entire stockade about twenty feet inside from it, over which if a man passes or reaches he becomes the mark of the two or three sentries nearest him. This rule is over diligently carried out, and it is very dangerous to approach the line. It is rumored that Grant has got into Petersburg. A man killed about two rods from us last night by falling into a well.

June 20th. Very hot till afternoon, when rain began and continued incessantly for several hours. Dyer is better, and I am troubled with the same disorder which he has had. I begin to wonder if I ever shall see home again.

June 21st. Warm as ever, with the usual shower in the afternoon. Another man is shot on the dead-line. Over one hundred men died to-day, but their places were more than made good by the prisoners from Sherman's army.

June 22d. Very hot. Rations of a pint of meal and a small piece of sow-belly. Hear the tantalizing report of an exchange of prisoners, to begin July 1st.

June 23d. Very hot. A lot of prisoners from Grant's army came in, taken at Petersburg. A great display of eggs, cucumbers, biscuit, squashes, potatoes, beans, and parsnips is seen, torturing the poor fellows who are dying by scores each day for want of these same luxuries. They are brought in by the rebel guard. There was the usual number of free fights in camp, where clubs, razors, and fists were freely used.

June 24th. Very warm. Drew rations of mush and sow-belly yesterday, and raw meal and salt to-day. We do not venture from under our shelter during the middle part of the day, when the torrid rays melt us quickly.

June 25th. Very hot. Rations of raw meal and meat, but no wood to cook them with, so we eat our meat raw. I had a good wash at the creek to-day, though without soap. Rows in camp are increasing, and it presents a scene like a second Babel.

June 26th. Prisoners from General Steele's army came in. I washed my pants in the creek. I am feeling quite weak from diarrhoea, which makes me desponding. This is the Sabbath; but how unlike our peaceful New England Sabbaths. Poor starved men of almost every nationality; many without a spark of principle, bounty-jumpers, New York "dead rabbits," Baltimore "plug-uglies," the sick and dying all around, make this a scene of horror which will be ever vivid in my memory, if I am allowed to see the end of all this. But every dark cloud has its silver lining, and I can trust God has us under his keeping.

June 27th. Two prisoners were brought in who tunneled out ten days ago and traveled over a hundred miles, living on sweet potatoes from plantations along their route. The blood-hounds overtook them near the Florida line, so they have returned to prison life, refreshed by pure air. Several shots were fired at men on the deadline.

June 28th. Hot. Heavy shower in the evening. Six hundred prisoners from Grant's army, taken near Petersburg, came in. Among them we found the familiar faces of [Thomas] Winn, [Thomas Stephens] Stevens, and [William H.] Tyler from the 21st. Thirty Indian sharp-shooters from Northern Michigan, also. I learn that my brother Henry is with the regiment, and is acting adjutant.

June 29th. A soldier from Ohio, who lay sick with fever within arm's-length of me, died in the night. Showers in the afternoon. Rations to-night two quarts of meal. It has been found that the outlaws in camp have formed a league, styling themselves "the raiders," and for the past two days matters have come to a terrible state. Two men murdered, one thrown into a deep well, and many knocked on the head and plundered, generally new arrivals, known to have money, watches, or other valuables. The rebel authorities have allowed the prisoners to form a police organization of several hundred men, who are armed with clubs and are hunting up the desperadoes. The afternoon has been one of great excitement, as twenty or thirty of the raiders have already been secured and sent out.

June 30th. Passed a sleepless night, for the police and raiders have kept up a continual fight, and this morning the camp is in the wildest excitement. The ringleader has not been found, but several of the raiders have been found buried under blankets with valuables to escape detection. At three in the afternoon, the ringleader was found under a pile of blankets and pine boughs. It was difficult to get him outside of the stockade unharmed. The rebels sent him immediately back to the tender mercies of his fellow-prisoners. Hardly had the gates closed upon him, as his trembling form reappeared, when the outraged prisoners fell upon and literally tore him to pieces: his carcase was carried out an unrecognizable mass. We feel that the ring is effectually broken up, although we are told that the rest are to be pardoned; but, if they are returned here, there will be no pardon for them.

July 1st. At noon an opening was made through the stockade into the new addition: and during the afternoon fifty detachments, or over thirteen thousand men, moved into it, ours among the number. We have now twenty-five acres enclosed, but the camp appears just as crowded as ever.

Jim Miller and I found a 34th Massachusetts man (Levi Shepard) who had a rubber blanket, so we three go in together: my woolen now serves for a shelter from the sun and rain, and Shep.'s rubber for the ground, so we are in more tolerable condition. There was some order planned in the arrangement of detachments into streets, but our allotted ground was much too small, so we are in as great a jumble as ever.

July 2d. Very hot. Found an old tent-mate of the 36th Massachusetts, who was taken near White House Landing, when on his way to his regiment on the 30th of May. Water is very difficult to get, and of poor and filthy quality. We drew two rations, owing to a misunderstanding on the part of the rebels. On account of the low state of our morals we did not return the extra ration.

July 3d. Very hot. Roll was called throughout the camp. Our detachment lost their rations on account of the absence of half a dozen men; so our extra rations of yesterday were very opportune.

July 4th. Very hot. We didn't celebrate the "glorious 4th" by feasting, but roasting half of our pint of meal for breakfast, made mush of the other half for dinner, and had raw pork for supper. The detachments were reorganized, and ours is now the 63d. In place of the usual fire-works in the evening, over thirty thousand filled the night air with songs of "John Brown's Body," "Star-Spangled Banner," "Down with the Traitors," etc., cheers for Vicksburg and Gettysburg victories of a year ago, and groans for Hog Winder and the Dutch Captain. All of which were given with an unction, and did not fail to reach the ears of those for whom they were intended.

July 5th. Very hot, but a fine breeze blows up from the swamp. A death from cholera last night is reported. Rumors of the fall of Richmond on the 2d.

July 6th. Very hot. More prisoners came in to-day. The camp is full of rumors of an exchange to begin to-morrow. Succeeded in getting an axe for a few moments and cut up some wood.

July 7th. Very hot. Several "wood riots" and knock-downs occurred. The quartermaster has issued axes to each detachment, thereby stopping the letting of axes at fifty and seventy-five cents an hour, which the blood-suckers have been practicing.

July 8th. Very warm. Several hundred prisoners from Grant's army and James Island came in, which made unusual commotion outside. One poor fellow of our squad died of diarrhea during the night. A large prayer-meeting was held near us, to which many a poor fellow delighted to crawl: every moment of the time was taken up in prayer, which went up from earnest hearts.

July 9th. Very hot, with a shower in the afternoon. Another man of our squad died to-day. A large number of prisoners from Hunter's West Virginia Army came in: they report a lot of prisoners from the 2d Corps on their way to this place. Washed shirt in creek.

July 10th. Very hot, with showers around us. More prisoners came in. The monotony of camp was broken by the parade of several camp-police with two or three prisoners, with their heads and faces shaved on one side, and a card attached to their backs bearing the word "Thief." They were greeted with brick-bats and cudgels as they passed along through the noisy, unsympathetic crowd.

July 11th. Another day of excitement. Seven hundred prisoners from Grant's army came in. After noon a scaffold was brought into camp, and erected near the south gate. At three the rebel camps were in commotion: the entire guard came out under arms, and were placed in line of battle at different points around camp, and the batteries were all manned. At four o'clock six of the condemned raiders were brought in under a strong guard of Union prisoners. After they had ascended the scaffold, a Catholic priest attended to their spiritual wants individually: meal-bags were tied over their heads and the ropes adjusted, while every living soul inside and outside the stockade was looking on in silence. At a given signal the six dropped off: five went struggling into eternity, while the rope of the sixth broke, and falling to the earth he gave a bound and was away like a frightened deer, over tents, and smashing in shanties; in his race of despair he reached the swamp, and after floundering about a few moments was re-taken. After begging most piteously for his life, he was taken up to the scaffold, and the second time launched off, this time into eternity. One man was from New York, one from New Jersey, one from Pennsylvania, and two were sailors. There is now a feeling of greater security than there has been for a long time, but may I never witness another scene like that!

July 12th. Showers around us have cooled the air and it is quite comfortable. Six hundred prisoners from Grant's army came in today, among them Allen from Baldwinsville, of the 36th Massachusetts. I bathed in the muddy creek in the evening. Prayer-meetings every pleasant evening and very largely attended.

July 13th. Very warm, but cloudy. An extra ration of rice was dealt out to all in camp. Two men were shot on the dead-line, and a third was fired at. There are now one hundred and ten full detachments of two hundred and seventy men each, in camp, besides the crowded hospitals outside.

July 14th. Warm in the forenoon, but cloudy in the afternoon. Several were shot on the dead-line during the day. The sergeants were ordered to appear at the gate, where they received the pleasing information that grape and canister would be fired into camp without further notice, if large crowds should collect or any unusual commotion occur. There was a general review of the camp guard outside, and a salute of two guns fired. The authorities evidently fear an uprising in camp.

July 15th. A few cripples and "bummers" from Sherman's army came in. The rebels are suspicious that large tunnels are in progress, and are hunting for them near the dead-line. A petition has been made up to send to our government, praying for a speedy release of all here. Death is doing his share of the work faithfully.

July 16th. Two tunnels have been discovered, one of them running fifty yards outside of the stockade, and would probably have been a great success, had the place not been betrayed by a fellow of the 7th Maine, who for the extra mess of pottage sold his brethren. Jim Miller has gone in with Osgood, so Shep. and I have the tent to ourselves.

July 17th. Very chilly last night, but warm to-day. The 7th Maine fellow was hunted down by the police and put to torture, after which his head was shaved, and with "traitor" on his back, he was most unmercifully beaten by the justly indignant prisoners. Rations of molasses in place of meat.

A.J. Riddle photograph looking southeast showing the sinks along the Stockade branch of Sweetwater creek.

July 18th. A man was shot near the dead-line by the *accidenta* discharge of a sentry's musket, and killed. Prisoners who came in to-day report Montgomery, Ala., burnt by a Union raiding party.

July 19th. Very hot. Hog Winder has allowed six men to go to Washington to present the petition for parole or exchange, the men to be appointed by a committee of twenty men inside the stockade. The Union raiding party is said to be steering for this place.

July 20th. The rebels seem to be thoroughly alarmed. Negroes are throwing up fortifications all around camp. Raw militia is being hurried in on the cars. Two prisoners were discovered escaping from the outside end of a tunnel and fired at; several others had already escaped.

July 21st. Sergeant Webster was disposed, Mumford succeeding him in charge of the detachment. The Johnnies are very active outside: trains have been running all day and night. A few prisoners taken near Atlanta came in. Another ration of molasses instead of meat,--a very poor substitute for those troubled with diarrhea.

July 22d. Three hundred prisoners from Grant's army came in, captured June 29th. Several tunnels partly dug were found. A sentry fired at a man near the dead-line, but missed him.

July 23d. Cloudy and comfortable. Rations of corn-bread, sow-belly, and salt. "Raiding" has been going on, and several fights, but the police are on the alert.

July 24th. Last night was very cold and to-day is very hot, which increases the mortality. Rations of rice and sow-belly.

July 25th. Last night was the coldest of the season. I could not sleep much, but laid awake listening to the coughs and groans from all directions. I have canker in my throat, which is painful. More tunnels were found. Rations of rice, but no salt to go with it. Water-melons, apples, eggs, doughnuts, berry pies, biscuit, etc., for sale in camp, but no one has any money. Cloudy and rain. I have taken cold, and my throat is quite sore. Rations of raw meal and sow-belly.

July 27th. Four hundred men from Grant and Sherman came in to-day. One was shot soon after coming in, while reaching under the dead-line for clear water,--probably not knowing the rules; his brains were blown into the water. I traded my ration of pork for cayenne pepper and used it for my throat, which is filling up with canker and very painful.

July 28th. Hot; shower in afternoon. I have great difficulty in talking and eating from the filling up in my throat. Seventeen hundred prisoners from Sherman came in, during which the rebels fired a solid shot a few feet over our heads, which struck in the marsh outside; it caused a big scare and dispersed the crowd in quick time. The fort around headquarters is nearly completed.

July 29th. Very hot. The usual shower in the afternoon. A line of white flags has been stationed through camp, marking the limit beyond which no crowd must collect. The rebels hardly dare put their threat into execution without modifying it. ----and---- went outside to work on their parole of honor. Two men of the 11th Massachusetts died near me.

July 30th. Very hot. Our rebel sergeant has called for shoemakers, and ---- sent in his name. The coarse, uncooked corn-meal has brought on the diarrhoea again.

July 31st. Very hot. The rebels have been felling trees all about camp to serve as a blockade. More rumors of exchange and parole. I have been suffering from a severe headache and fever turn.

August 1st. Very hot; rain last night. I was sick all night, but feel better this morning. A preacher from outside held services in camp, and read the exchange report in the newspaper. Ambulances have been taking out sick all the afternoon.

August 2d. Very hot. Heavy thunder-shower in the afternoon, which flooded us all, soaking everything. I am quite sick,--very weak from cough and diarrhea. A lot of prisoners came in, who report that they were taken at Macon while *en route* for this place to relieve us. The sick have been going out all day.

August 3d. Very hot. The moving of the sick to the outside has been going on all day, causing much talk and rumor as to the why and wherefore.

August 4th. Very hot. No sick were taken out; neither roll-call nor sick-call took place. One of our squad died near me this noon. Prayer-meeting was held near me in the evening.

August 5th. Very hot. All the sick of the first eight detachments were taken out. Prisoners from Sherman came in. I was taken with a severe headache at night. We are continually tormented and tantalized with the sight of peaches, apples, chickens, and soda-water offered for sale at fabulous prices.

August 6th. Very warm. The dread monotony of our miserable life is broken only by the hundreds of rumors of exchange, causing renewed disappointment to the believing. A man was killed on the dead-line, and another shot at in the evening.

August 7th. Very warm. Several convalescents came in from the hospitals, and report an awful condition of affairs there. I am feeling better, except an irritating cough. Prisoners from Sherman came in.

August 8th. A row of sheds inside camp at the west end are being built for the sick. Rain all the afternoon.

August 9th. Very warm. The heaviest thunder shower of the season occurred in the afternoon, which flooded camp and undermined the stockade in several places so that it fell over, causing wild excitement among the authorities outside. All the guard were called by the long roll, the batteries all manned and turned on us poor fellows, who were greatly amused by their alarm. Four hundred prisoners from Sherman came in. Poor old Boyer, a German from Ohio, died near me. All day yesterday and last night he lay, almost within arm's-length of me, moaning and crying for water, while every draught seemed to throw him into spasms; and when he died we all felt relieved that rebel hate could do no more to him. In the evening I went over and had a good talk of old times with Walter Lamb.

August 10th. Heavy shower in the afternoon. The rebels worked all day very lively on the stockade. Drew half rations of bread, raw beans, and fresh meat, but no wood. I feel well to-day, but mighty hungry. The wet weather causes rapidly-increasing mortality.

August 11th. Very warm; rain in the afternoon. The rancid bacon, flinty corn-bread, and beans that are not all beans, make us dainty. The beans come to us cooked up with all sorts of chaff, dirt, and bean-bugs, but it all fills up, and we ought to be grateful. Prisoners came in from Sherman. The old stockade is all up, and the negroes are at work erecting another one twenty rods outside, so that tunneling will have to be dispensed with.

August 12th. Rations of bread (half-cooked), rice (quarter-cooked), meat (slightly warmed). More prisoners from Sherman to-day.

August 13th. Very hot and clear. Beautiful moonlight evening. We have two new neighbors from Iowa, who have stretched their blankets with ours. They were taken in the rear of Johnson's army, while raiding. They were robbed of a large amount of money, and of watches and clothing. The bank of the creek has been boarded up, so that we are able to dip for water without making it muddy. Shower in the evening; our rations better to-night.

August 14th. Prisoners from Sherman to-day report Atlanta taken by our forces.

August 15th. Very hot. Headache at night. Rations smaller than ever.

August 16th. Very hot, with shower in the evening. Two years ago to-day I sold myself to Uncle Sam to help "put down the rebellion." This day finds the tables turned, and the accursed rebellion trying to put me down. It remains to be seen whether all this wholesale persecution of the helpless will avail to establish a new and honored government at the south.

August 17th. Very hot, which makes my head ache constantly. I found a book on temperance, which I have been reading,--the first I have seen, except my little testament, since my capture.

August 18th. Very hot. A new rebel sergeant called our roll, who finds it difficult to read writing, and in his haste does not get answers to many of the names. The rations of the supposed absentees are consequently cut off. I am down sick with diarrhea and headache. More prisoners from Sherman come in.

August 22d. To-night finds me better able to write. I feel that I have been very near to death's door. The weather has continued hot as ever, and my diarrhea, which took the form of dysentery, made me nearly helpless. Then my head ached till I thought I should become crazy. I thought of the regiment as the 19th of August came round, when I suppose they were to be mustered out. My spirits went down to zero as I thought of the prospect of my old comrades compared with my own. Oh, that the old pale horse would not stare me in the face so hard and so constantly. Yesterday I felt that my pluck had nearly vanished, and it seemed as if the only hold on life which I had was in the comfort derived from the precious words which I read, "My son, despise not thou the chastening of the Lord, nor faint when thou art rebuked of Him, for whom the Lord loveth He chasteneth." Shep. has been very kind, and I feel thankful that my prayers have been answered and I am really better. The mortality on these cold, wet nights is terrible. A large prayer-meeting was held on the flat in the evening. Rations of corn-bread, beans, and molasses.

August 23d. Very hot all day and night; mosquitoes very troublesome. [E] Baker, of the 34th Massachusetts, of our mess, and another member of the 34th, died to-night, near by. Prisoners from Kilpatrick came in.

August 24th. Very hot. I am feeling much stronger. Shep. went outside to the dead-house with a dead body. When he returned, after a stay of some ten minutes, he seemed greatly refreshed. Another man close by us died to-night. Some commissioned officers, disguised as privates, were taken out and sent away.

August 25th. Very hot. Rations of raw beans and beef. A few prisoners came in.

August 26th. This roasting hot weather does much toward driving men to idiocy. Many a poor fellow has been sun-struck, and gone up. This is what drives the humanity out of us. Rations of bread (a morsel), sow-belly (a bit), molasses (plenty), salt (a particle). Funeral services were held over a dead comrade near my tent, which seemed civilized.

August 27th. Very warm, but a good breeze which keeps the dust stirring. Rebs report heavy fighting at Petersburg on the 19th, when Grant was defeated.

August 28th. "Macon Telegraph" gives notice of a general exchange; but thanks that I am beyond believing anything now till the Stars and Stripes are between me and this hell on earth.

August 29th. Prisoners from Sherman yesterday and to-day.

August 30th. Warm and clear. Last night was cold and uncomfortable. Providence opened a new spring during the heavy shower of a day or two since, washing away a large stream of pure cold water flowing out, which supplies a large part of the camp. The man is a fool who doubts a kind and benevolent Providence after such a manifestation.

September 1st. Drew microscopic rations of beef, bread, ham, beans, and salt; some detachments had rice in place of bread.

September 2d. Last two nights have been uncomfortably cold. I have been a prisoner three months. How dreary the prospect ahead.

September 3d. Cloudy, with northeast wind. A crowd of convalescents came in from outside, and a lot of sick went out. In the afternoon there was a great stir in camp on account of the arrival of a mail from the north. [German] Lagara, the Frenchman, of Company K, received a letter from his wife, and the generous soul has been reading it to us greedy ones who receive none. Sherman is reported to have got in the rear of Hood.

September 4th. Mild. I read a letter written from Templeton, Mass., to Wilber Potter, in which I learn that Colonel [George P.] Hawkes has resigned and gone home; also that ----- has become a Christian. This was all; but no one but those in our situation can realize the pleasure of hearing even this and seeing a letter from home. Clark, of our squad, died to-night, and [Waldo] Dwinnell, of Company G, went out to the hospital, and I presume we shall never see him again, as his strength is all gone, and he is very badly emaciated.

September 5th. Very hot. Drew rations of rice and molasses, bread and pork, which we found to be a mistake, as squad three lost theirs, so most of our boys gave up their extra.

September 6th. The whole camp is wild with excitement over the prospect of exchange, for the first eighteen detachments are now under marching orders. Nobody understands it, but there is a universal uplifting of heads by those who had already shut out hope.

September 7th. Very hot. Ten detachments were taken out. Ten more ordered to be in readiness. Drew a pint of meal, and pork. Holshoult, of the 34th Massachusetts, of our squad, died to-night.

September 8th. Cloudy. Mosquitoes troublesome. Several detachments left during the night, and a large number to-day. Rations of raw meal and beans.

September 9th. All the sick have been moved into the sheds at the west end. Prisoners from Sherman came in, and many went away at night. Rations of bread and meal, but no salt.

September 10th. Rourke, of our squad, died to-night, and I was detailed to carry him out to the dead-house. This is the first time I have been outside these horrid gates since I came in three months ago; and 'tho' outside less than three minutes, I caught a breath of fresh air which gave me a new lease on life. Rations of rice, meal, and molasses, and no salt. Several detachments went out at night and in the morning. Forty detachments have now gone, and camp looks quite deserted; though there are over twenty thousand still here.

September 11th. There is a beautiful harvest moon shining down upon us. I wonder if dear friends at home are looking at it also and thinking of me. Ten detachments left to-night. Nearly all the 21st boys have left, Miller among the number. How homesick it makes a fellow feel to see all his friends leaving him in a place like this.

September 12th. Graton stopped with us last night. Eighteen detachments go out to-day.

September 13th. A large number of "flankers" from our squad got out last night with those who went away, so that our rations are larger in consequence. Go it, boys, while you can. To-night we receive orders to be in readiness to start in the morning.

September 14th. Very hot. The train which left last night collided with a freight train six miles away, by which eight of the cars were smashed, killing and wounding about sixty "Northern Mudsills." All of the uninjured on that train were sent back into camp, and none left to-day.

September 15th. Days hot and nights cold. 1,100 sick sent away to-day. 2,000 of Sherman's men ordered to be ready to leave on a special exchange, for which reason we do not get our rations till late in the night. A heavy shower in the afternoon.

September 16th. Hot. A large number of sick have been going out all day. 600 of yesterday's batch returned to camp for want of transportation.

September 17th. Cloudy; heavy rain at night. 700 men of Sherman's exchange left, several of them from our detachment. It seems lonely and drear to see the thousands of deserted burrows and dens.

September 18th. Stormy. No prisoners went out; and no signs of any more going at present,--many long faces in consequence. Shep. is sick with the diarrhea.

September 19th. Cloudy; rain at night. ---and---sent into camp because two or three of their comrades ran away. They say that it is supposed that the prisoners have only been transferred to other prisons, Charleston and Savannah. 1,100 more of Sherman's exchange went out; each man' name called to prevent "flankers."

September 20th. Cloudy; rain in the night. Signs of scurvy have appeared in my mouth; am feeling very poorly. Drew no bread to-day.

September 21st. Cloudy and rain. Very chilly and damp nights. Great numbers sick with colds. Drew a ration of mouldy sea-biscuit, molasses and beans. Bad as the bread was it was a desirable change from the "grits."

September 22d. Sun came out scorching hot at noon, and shower in the afternoon. The camp has been reorganized into new detachments of 240 men each, divided into four squads of sixty men each. They number from forty-five to seventy-three: ours is the seventy-second.

September 23d. Shower in the afternoon. A lively trade between the guard and prisoners: the prisoners' articles of traffic being military buttons, and the rebs' sweet potatoes. Some rebel officers visiting here rode around the dead-line to view the human menagerie.

September 24th. Several showers during the day. Washed in the creek. Ration of raw meal.

The Dutch captain has been inspecting the ration wagons, and tells us we are entitled to more rations than we get. Oh, well, don't we know it!

September 25th. Clear and mild. It was so cold we could not sleep last night. We are beginning to realize that we must remain here through the winter. Will hope keep us up much longer?

September 26th. Roll-call; and all men not in line were deprived of their rations. Prisoners who came in from Sherman say that the special exchange is true, but no general exchange. The chief quartermaster has been inspecting us. Wonder how he likes the looks!

September 27th. Roll was called, and men put into our detachment to fill up the places of flankers. Our ration of beans very small, and the most filthy we ever had: dirt, bugs, worms, chaff, and pods being the principle ingredients. The shout was raised "fall in," and several more detachments were sent away, but ours will be the last, so our case is well-nigh hopeless. More prisoners from Sherman came in.

September 28th. Warm and comfortable last night. Drew rations of meal, beef, beans, wood, pork, salt, and molasses, which were dealt out to us in crumbs, drops, splinters, and teaspoonfuls. Three and a half detachments went out to-day.

September 29th. I found a "History of the World" by Peter Parley, which has been a rare treat to me for the hour or more allowed me to keep it. Drew very small rations of meal, beans, and beef. Five more detachments prepared to leave, but the train did not come for them.

September 30th. Very warm and sultry. At roll-call all detachments were filled up. Drew molasses in place of meat, a very poor substitute for these hungry starving skeletons. Tasted a sweet potato, which was a great luxury. A ration of a teaspoonful of soft soap was distributed throughout camp, and nobody knows what to do with it.

October 1st. Washed in the creek, just to use up the soap: *that was all.* Rations of bread and beans. A train-load of prisoners went away.

October 2d. Four months a prisoner, and oh, how long ones! A few Sherman prisoners, captured near Atlanta, came in. Drew a splendid ration of beans. We find it difficult to remember the Sabbath as it comes round, but conclude that this is one up in God's country, if we haven't lost our reckoning.

October 3d. Heavy showers. Several men went to work on their parole of honor as teamsters, choppers, etc.

October 4th. Another load of prisoners went away this evening, among whom were [Alvin S.] Granton and [George V.] Barker of the 21st. Two shots were fired on the dead-line.

October 5th. I was detailed to "pack" the sick and dead, to and from the sheds, for which I drew an extra ration of bread, rice, and molasses. My teeth and jaws are quite sore.

October 6th. Cloudy and rain. My sleep was broken by teethache. I trade away my ration of meal for beans, which I eat as dry as possible to check the progress of scurvy. Rations to-day of bread, beans, bacon, beef, and molasses, just enough to keep life in the lice and fleas, which companions in misery stick closer than brothers.

October 7th. Cloudy and damp. Had a suffering night from my teeth. Shep. is sick, as also many others, with chills and ague.

October 8th. The weather changed suddenly in the night, and to-day is clear and cold. Lost another night's sleep from teethache. Many poor fellows are sinking, and dying from exposure to this hard weather.

October 9th. Still clear and cold. We are moved over to the south end of this deserted camp, and are formed into detachments of five hundred men in each. We are in the 4th. Shep. and I dug a hole in the ground, over which we spread our blanket, for another cold night is expected, and we must work to keep from getting a death-chill, even if it is the Sabbath.

October 10th. Spent a suffering and sleepless night. The coldest night of the season. The rebel guards on their elevated posts suffered from the freezing wind and were impatient to get off, and very noisy all night. There are now about 2,500 men in camp. Shep. and I mess with Sergeant Phelps, of Vermont, and twenty others. Teeth ache all day.

October 11th. Mild. Spent a more comfortable night. The sick at the sheds get hard tack. Three hundred prisoners from Sherman came in, captured between Atlanta and Marietta.

October 12th. My jaws are very sore. The entire camp was kept in line all the morning while the sergeants arranged the rolls, and the quartermaster arranged the camp into streets. A new dead-line was put up.

October 13th. More arranging and moving about. We now lie very compact; about three thousand men occupying about three acres, two thirds of which space is included in the streets. I have been peddling coffee at the hospital sheds, made from burnt meal.

October 14th. Cloudy and cool. Spent another night of suffering. Men at work fixing up their tents for winter. Quite a large number of sick were admitted to the sheds. Street sutlers are plenty, with an abundance of sweet potatoes and biscuit for sale.

October 15th. Shep. and I have been digging our grave deeper, over which we spread our blanket. Teeth ache all day another sleepness night.

October 16th. I was detailed to "pack" dead out to the dead-house from the sheds. I carried out two men belonging to the 19th Massachusetts. Nights are cold and frosty, and no wood to keep warm with.

October 17th. Large details have been made to go out for wood. Rations of raw beans and molasses, but no bread. Made candy of my molasses. Rain in the evening.

October 18th. I went outside the stockade for wood; and oh how like a new life it seemed to see the green grass and leaves, and breathe the fresh air, and be surrounded by sights and smells which no one can ever appreciate as fully as those who live as we do. It gives me a new longing to live, and also a new torture in the doubt and hopeless look of the future. Shep. and I have been writing letters home, sending for boxes. Several convalescents tried to escape from the hospitals, but the hounds caught them.

October 19th. Shep. sick with diarrhea. Rations of rice and molasses.

October 20th. Warmer last night. Went out for wood again, so we have a fire to sit by this evening. Beans and beef for to-day's rations.

October 21st. Pleasant day, but cold night. Several went to the hospital from our mess, Webster among the number. Rations of rice and molasses in place of beans and beef.

October 22d. Shep. and I have fixed up blankets with Laird of Pennsylvania, by which means we get an extra blanket for nights.

October 23d. Very cold and heavy frost last night, for which could not sleep much. Went out again for wood.

October 24th. Had a comfortable night's rest. We think we have our tent made very comfortable. The chief sutler was cleaned out by the Dutch captain for selling liquor, and his goods confiscated for the benefit of the sick about camp.

October 25th. The wood detail has been stopped because some of the men have escaped. Salt is very scarce.

October 26th. An order confiscating all salt offered for sale in camp has been issued by the Dutchman, Teeth ache very severely.

October 27th. Stormy. Our tent was flooded. I am hoarse and used up generally for want of sleep. Rations of bread and rice, very small, barely enough to sustain life.

October 28th. Hard toothache and poor night's rest. Washed in the creek and mended shirt. Traded off my ration of beans for an excellent ration of rice. A mud shanty fell in, breaking one man's back and badly crippling two others.

October 29th. Very cold, and heavy frost last night. Toothache very severe. Fixed up our tent so that it is weather-proof. Six prisoners came in.

October 30th. Had about an hour's sleep last night. Shep. applied for admission to the hospital, but was refused. The whole camp has received orders to be ready to march.

October 31st. Warm and lowering. First, second, and part of third detachment went away in the morning, but there is no enthusiasm, for we believe it to be only a change of prisons, the report of exchange being only a dodge of the rebels to keep us from any attempt to escape during transportation. The rebel sergeants have been taking our carpenters to work on their parole of honor. Rations of bread and rice cooked without a particle of salt.

November 1st. The sheds are being cleared of all sick, who are either taken outside or returned to camp.

November 2d. Storm commenced before midnight, and rained hard about twelve hours; fortunately for us our tent was kept quite dry, while most of the others were flooded. This is about the last of Andersonville for us, and it is a general abandoning of this horrid place. Orders came for us all to be ready to start at eleven A.M., but transportation did not arrive, and we did not start until ten at night, when we were roused out of a sound sleep, and went through the gates in perfect darkness and in a pelting rain, thus passing out of a place which, however long we live, will always combine more of the realities to be expected in that dark and terrible region of despair of the future world known as "hell," than any other can to us. In the pitchy darkness we were packed into old freight cars (eighty-three in a car), the doors were shut and secured, and we were soon moving towards Macon.

November 3d. Packed as we were, it was impossible to change position, and I sat all night on the bottom of the car, with hardly a wink of sleep. Passing through Macon at daylight, we continued our journey on the Charleston Railroad, riding all day and until late at night, in the same cramped sitting posture; at last we arrived at Millen Station, two hundred miles from Andersonville, in a pitable condition, and found great relief in getting out and stretching our aching limbs. One of my mess died in our car on the trip. Marching half a mile, we came to another stockade, and camped outside for the rest of the night.

November 4th. Clear, but very cold wind. Suffered for want of shelter and clothes. We were formed into detachments as before, and marched inside, where we drew rations of rice, meal, beef, beans, and salt. Camped by the side of the creek. Find this place nice, clean, and roomy, though about ten thousand of our old prisoners are here.

November 5th. Drew two days' rations, better in quantity and quality than at Andersonville; but suffer for want of shelter. Those who came in first have made comfortable winter-quarters of logs. Several hundred, in despair of exchange, have taken the oath, and gone into the rebel army.

November 6th. Chilly. Couldn't sleep last night on account of the cold. Laird and I went out for wood.

November 7th. Warm night. Found Lamb and Graton. Made a temporary shelter. The man who hung the raiders last summer was chased out of camp by part of the old ring, but he escaped unharmed.

November 8th. Light rain. I had a comfortable night's sleep. This is supposed to be presidential election day, and a great deal of excitement and sport was made in voting for the two candidates, Little Mac and Old Abe. My vote proved to have been cast for the triumphant candidate in camp. Abraham received a majority of nine hundred and seventy-five in a total casting of over nine thousand.

November 9th. I went out for wood twice to-day. A great cheering outside among the rebels, which the guard told us was caused by the news of a general exchange.

November 10th. Rain in the morning. Cold and windy at night. An inspecting officer has been taking the names of those most ragged in camp, for clothing.

November 11th. Clear and cold. A recruiting officer has been in camp enticing prisoners to enlist in the rebel army. Several went from our division.

November 12th. Very chilly wind all day. Our two days' rations did not come till late at night, because a number of the enlisted recruits could not be found, and the authorities feared that they had been murdered by our boys, who are very indignant at their action. A man near me, who was nearly naked, perished with the cold.

November 13th. Chilly wind and frosty night. Names of sick, seventy-five from each division, were taken to the surgeons, who examined and passed them out, to be sent to Savannah for exchange. Shepard and Graton were examined and passed; they expect to go to-morrow. What an inducement to be sick!

November 14th. Coldest night of the fall. Received a ration of sweet potatoes in place of meal, and of hard soap. I wrote a letter home, to send by Shepard.

November 15th. Shepard and his crowd left us. It did me good to see him go, though my heart sank to feel that I must always be left behind.

November 16th. Sweet potatoes were issued again. Another train of sick arrived from Andersonville. Our sick did not get away, and all returned inside the stockade to-day.

November 18th. A new sergeant, who could not read very well, called our roll, and did not get through so that we could draw our rations, till after dark; so we starve on three spoonfuls of rice all day. Shepard's lot of sick went away this time, and the surgeons are examining in camp for another load.

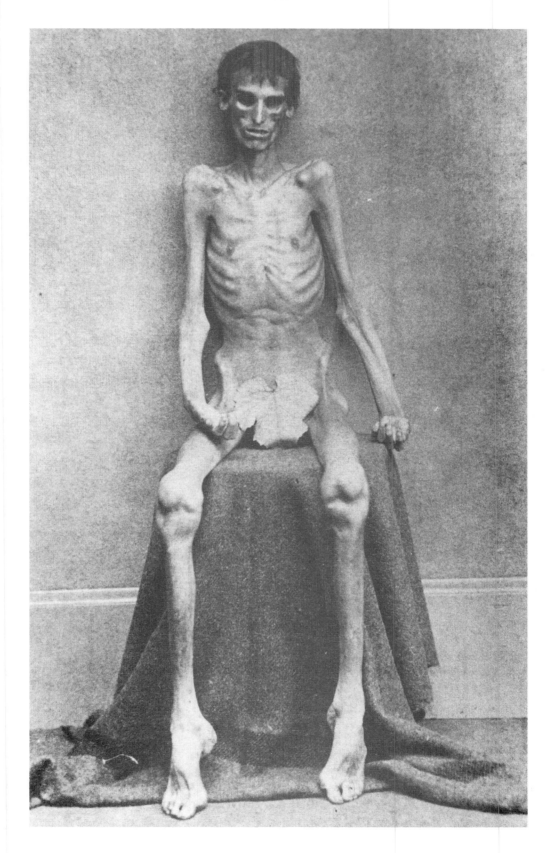

A living-skeleton survivor of Confederate prisons.

November 19th. Storm came on at night. Another change of sergeants, which caused another day's starvation on a mouthful of beef. Another train load of sick went away at dark.

November 20th. More sick were examined and passed out. At midnight the cry went around: "Fall in 1st and 2d divisions," and they packed up and went away.

November 21st. Stormed all day. At one o'clock at night we took possession of a fine shanty, abandoned by second division fellows, of which we enjoyed the occupancy until night, when we were ordered to pack up, and start off in the rain. Rumors are rife among the prisoners that Sherman has something to do with it, and our suspicions are confirmed when we reach the depot and see train after train pass down towards Savannah, loaded with all kinds of household goods, men with their families, and negroes of all ages, while numberless teams of all descriptions are depositing their freight alongside the railroad. We, meanwhile, stand in a terrible, freezing biting wind for hours, waiting for transportation, until at last, more dead than alive, chilled to the heart, we go on the cars (sixty in a car).

November 22d. At four o'clock in the morning we glided away through the pine forests toward Savannah, over one of the smoothest railroads I ever was on. Arriving at Savannah at sunset, we passed through the beautiful city and left the cars at dark. The weather was biting cold, no quarters or fuel were furnished us, and having had no rations for two days, most of us are too weak to move about and keep our blood stirring. A remaining spark of Yankee ingenuity suggested rather a novel mode of keeping warm. Two or three men would sit down on the ground, locking and interlacing each other in their arms and legs, while others would pack on and against them until there would be a solid stack of humanity of twenty, more or less. But in spite of every effort to keep warm, several of our poor, thin-blooded fellows froze to death.

November 24th. Milder than yesterday. Beef and salt were issued to us. Citizens have been bringing in food and clothes all, day, but I am not smart enough to get any. A lot of prisoners went south on the Florida road; the sick were also taken away, and the rest of us were allowed to get wood from the lumber-yard, with which we keep more comfortable at night.

November 25th. Clear. The kind-hearted people of Savannah continued to bring in food and clothing all day. I got some rice, which kept me till the rations of hard-tack and molasses came at dark. A train came along at nine in the evening, and we were hurried on board the cars. A rebel officer told us we were going to Charleston to be exchanged.

November 26th. After riding all night we find ourselves at sunrise approaching Charleston, cross the broad Cooper and Ashley rivers, and reach the city. Our cars stand in the streets all the forenoon, while many spectators came to see the Andersonville pack. In the afternoon we are run about five miles out of the city, and change cars, our only exchange at Charleston. Moving northward we rode until ten o'clock, when we left the cars at Florence, one hundred miles from Charleston.

November 27th. Having spent the night in bivouac by the side of the railroad, in the morning our names are taken and we are sent inside another stockade, which we find crowded with old prisoners from Andersonville. Laird and I spread our blankets together, and at night drew a ration of meal and flour, which, by the aid of a few chips, we made a supper of; and though our hopes had been checked by this termination of "the exchange," still the change of air and scene has stimulated us somewhat, and we do not feel ready to say die yet.

November 28th. After a cheerless, sleepless night on the cold, damp ground, I got a breakfast of flour paste, and found all the old comrades of the 21st--Miller, Middy, and all well. This camp is crowded fully as badly as Andersonville was; the location is damp and swampy, and the rations poorer and smaller than ever. The sick from each thousand are being paroled each day.

November 29th. I bought some straw with a borrowed $5 confederate scrip; and mended my clothes, which are in a miserable condition: the sleeves of my blouse and shirt are almost entirely gone, showing some skeleton arms, the backs of both garments are as thin as gauze, while my pants are worn from the knees down, entirely away, and my cap is two simple pieces of cloth sewed together. I was detailed to go out for wood. Rations of a pint and a half of flour and a splinter of green gum-wood. More prisoners came from Millen.

November 30th. Had the chills last night and lost my sleep. Jim Miller was admitted to the hospital. Bathed in the creek. Rations of a pint and a half of meal, with beans and salt.

December 1st. All the prisoners were moved to one side of the creek, and then the entire camp made to move back to the other side again, being counted as they passed across the little bridge. A lot of "galvanized Yanks"--turncoats--were sent back into camp by the rebels for fear they would escape to our army.

December 2d. Six months a prisoner.

December 3d. Roll-call and wood rations were omitted "on account of the return of a large number of paroled sick," though we don't see the relation of cause and effect. I traded a map of the seat of war for a mess of sweet potatoes.

December 4th. The prisoners were again transferred back and forth in order to get a correct count. I copied a map of the States of North and South Carolina, which for *unexplained reasons* has become a favorite occupation among certain prisoners. Rations of a pint of rice. A sick man was shot dead on the dead-line.

December 5th. Frosty night, but beautiful to-day. I drew a ration of a pint and a half of meal, but no wood to cook with.

December 6th. Foggy in the morning; clear and cold at night. I heard preaching from clergyman from Florence. Went out for wood.

December 8th. Very chilly and cloudy. I am not prepared to understand my situation yet, so unexpectedly has it come upon me. In the morning the remaining four thousand in camp were called out into the dead-line and examined. Laird and I were near the last end of one of the lines. As the rebel surgeon came along, glancing at one and another, speaking to perhaps one out of a dozen, he passed me by,--an incident which did not attract my attention much, as I had no idea I was worth noticing any how. But he turns and looks back at me, and then steps back, asks my condition, examines me more closely, thumps me (and my heart thumps back), asks the name of my regiment, State, time of expiration of term of service, and then, turning away, says abruptly, "You may go." No words will ever strike me as those did; asking him to repeat them--not fully understanding--I bounded out of the stockade as if I had been shot out. Hardly was I out and looking about me, when I saw Laird following me. Too overjoyed to think of anything else, we clasped each other's hands and cried like babies. Found and signed our parole papers, after which we were sent out on a large level field, with a number of others, without much guard, all day and night. Rations of meal and sweet potatoes.

December 9th. Cloudy and cold. Suffered severely, as the small fires could not afford us, bloodless creatures, much warmth, and we were nearly blinded with smoke. At night our names were called, each of us drew *a loaf of wheat bread*, and before it was dark all of us (one thousand in all) were on board a long train of rickety, broken cars. Pain in all my joints, cold and shaking, blind almost as a bat in the daylight, after being pulled into a car I laid down to wonder if death were not then really creeping over me.

December 10th. After an all-night ride, with some sleep, reached Charleston at eight o'clock in the morning, and left the cars in the lower part of the city near the mouth of the Ashley River. The day was cold and cloudy, and a dense mist hung over the harbor. We were kept a large part of the day on a wharf, waiting for the fog to clear away, exposed to the piercing winter's wind as it blew in from over the harbor. By the middle of the afternoon the mist had lifted, and at four P.M. we were transferred to a small steamer and sailed down the harbor. Passing the many points of interest which, under ordinary circumstances, would have commanded the closest attention of all, at this time all eyes were peering with intensest gaze out into the thick haze which hung over the harbor. At last old, ragged Fort Sumter came in view, and as we passed close under its ruined, battered walls, all eyes for a moment turned toward that historic pile. Then the boat's speed slackened, and swung slowly around so that the gaze of the prisoners, who were confined on the stern of the vessel, suddenly took in the sight before them. There, high before us, only a few yards away, lay the majestic steamer "City of New York," from whose topmast waved the grand old Stars and Stripes. The scene which follows beggars description. Men shouted and cheered, laughed like idiots, and cried like babies. Men stood with their eyes riveted on that flag as if dreaming; others danced or grasped each other, and all acted like madmen.

Transferred and exchanged! the fulfillment of "hopes long deferred."

A collection of Andersonville relics (buckets, sieves, cups, spoons, a checkerboard, etc.) including the grave marker #7606, of Sgt. Darius Starr, Co. F, 2nd U.S. Sharpshooters, captured on May 6, 1864 at the Wilderness, and died on September 2nd.

Private Manlius Comey, Co. F, 1st Massachusetts Heavy Artillery, was captured on June 22, 1864 near Petersburg, Va., and was imprisoned at Andersonville and later Florence, S.C. He was exchanged on December 8th, but died on the Transport "City of New York" before reaching Annapolis, Md.

Part Seven
"Death rather than dishonor."

Memoirs of J.N. Sweeny, Harrison B. Bennett, Henry Devilliz, A.S. Clyne

J.N. SWEENY
Company H, 8th Kansas Infantry

On December 8, 1864, I was put in charge of forty sick and dying comrades who were packed in a box-car at Florence, S.C., to be sent to Charleston for exchange. My duty was to attend to their various wants during the journey. Among the number was a poor emaciated skeleton, scarcely able to sit up. He was an old man, perhaps fifty. I noticed that he was trying to attract my attention by means of signs, but I did not understand them. He then showed me a small book--a work on Masonry--which he carried, and asked me if I knew anything about it. I told him I did not. This circumstance made him an object of my especial care during the trip. At Charleston we were put aboard the truce boat. I wrapped him in his old ragged blanket and carried him aboard. When we were transferred from the truce boat to a U.S. transport, I laid him down on the deck. He lay in such a position that the flag was in full view, flying at the masthead. He uncovered his face and looked full five minutes straight at the emblem of liberty, then, throwing up both hands, exclaimed: "Hurrah! hurrah! hurrah!" three times, and fell back a corpse. The next day we buried him in the Atlantic. That cry is still ringing in my ears. Would that I had language to describe that grand exhibition of loyalty and its effect upon those who witnessed it. If some of the stay-at-home cowards--who bushwacked us in the rear, and are still bushwacking us--had witnessed it, they would then be able to form correct opinions concerning the motives which prompted the soldier to choose death rather than dishonor. I have seen many die of hunger, while clutching between their emaciated fingers the moldy crust of bread at which their stomachs revolted, who could have life, liberty and plenty, by forswearing their allegiance to the flag. The men who braved the terrors of Andersonville were made of sterner stuff than to strike their colors to even that grim monster, Famine.

Private Thomas McQuilkin, Co. I, 1st Ohio Infantry, was captured on September 19, 1863 at Chickamauga, Ga., and was confined at Belle Isle, Richmond, Va., on September 29th. In March, 1864 he was sent to Andersonville. McQuilkin entered the hospital at Andersonville on August 6th and died October 23, 1864 of "Scorbutus". Grave # 11,341.

Gen. John Winder (left), Capt. Henry Wirz (right).

HARRISON B. BENNETT
Company C, 20th Ohio Infantry, Seventeenth Corps.
Age: 19.

I was captured, with 57 of my regiment, July 22, 1864, in front of Atlanta, Ga. We arrived at Andersonville about July 26. When unloaded from the cars we were marched some distance from the station and then halted by the notable Capt. Wirz. There was my first view of and experience with that old Dutchman. He commenced to count off a certain number of men from the front rank. He wanted to fill the ranks of the broken 90's--where men had died. I was the last one he wanted. He ordered us to step forward, and as I was the only one of my company he had taken I turned to say good-by to the boys. I chanced to raise my eyes, and the old devil was going after his ever ready navy, and had it almost level with my head. I moved up quite lively. He did not say a word, but put the gun back in its holster and marched us to his headquarters and there assigned us to different 90's. My luck was good then; I was assigned to the second 90, which had a reasonably good well of water, of which no one could get a drop unless he belonged to that 90. I was supplied with drinking water for myself and slipped quite a good deal to my company boys for drinking purposes.

Again I was fortunate, for my 90 drew rations the next morning, while the new 90's did not until the following morning.   After I was assigned and had received instructions as to being counted, drawing rations, etc., I started to take in the sights of the stockade.

Such sights as I beheld!   Oh, no pen, no tongue, no painter, can portray the scenes of human suffering and wretchedness that everywhere met our eyes in the Sheol!   I wandered, dazed and bewildered, among that multitude of starving, half-naked captives; pale, gaunt, haggard, wasted by disease and hunger, their scanty garments in rags; many without shelter from sun and rain and chilling dews.   They gave ghastly evidence of man's inhumanity to man.   I saw emaciated men struggling around slender fires to cook their meager rations of meal, or scraping bare beef bones to their last vestige of nutriment.

I saw them huddling under tattered blankets to shield them from the fierce noonday heat, or creeping like burrowing beasts into their holes in the ground.   I saw fellow-soldiers with hollow eyes, weak, helpless and devoured by vermin, borne on blankets to the dead-house.

I heard the shrieks and the curses of those whose gnawing misery had bereft them of moral volition and made them brutes.   I heard the groans of despair from men who had lived this hideous life through many wretched months, and in whose minds scarce a flickering spark of hope remained.

To relate the horrible scenes I beheld in that place would demand the space of many volumes. Language is futile, and words have lost their meaning when attempt is made to depict the bitter agony of body and mind and heart that often made death a welcome relief in that hell upon earth.

I returned to the spot where my company boys had selected their habitation and sat down, convinced that I could not live through such conditions as I had seen; in fact I had quite given up hope and was in despair, when my friend and dear comrade, John A. Fissell, came along.   I was sitting on the ground with my head resting on my knees when John asked what ailed me.   I told him what I had seen and that I had given up hope.

Then and there I received a lecture from John, and a lesson I shall never forget.   He cuffed me and kicked me and used language that he never learned at Sabbath School: "Get up!" said he, "and don't let me see you in that position any more!"   I am determined they shall not kill me here!   I propose to get out of this scrape and to pay them for such treatment."   I got up and made a similar resolve myself, and fought the battle through to the end.

Harrison Bennett died on April 30, 1923, age 78.

A.S. CLYNE
63rd New York State Volunteers

I belonged to the Sixty-third New York S.V., Second Brigade, First Division, Second Army Corps, and was captured at Petersburg, Va. We arrived in Andersonville on June 27th, and no one, except those who were there, can form any idea what my feelings were when we were ordered into line in front of the stockade by Capt. Wirz, the commander of the prison, who took our names, company and regiment. We were then all marched through the south gate of the stockade. I shall never forget the sight which presented itself to my view. Men with nothing on but a pair of worn-out drawers, bareheaded, in a broiling sun, and reduced to living skeletons, flocked around us to inquire what was the news in "God's Country;" how the Union army was getting along, or if we had a chew of tobacco, or a button for them--for buttons with the shanks were highly prized by the guards. A shudder went through me as I glanced around, and I wondered if ever I should be as wretched as my questioners. As I stood pondering what to do and how to act, a poor fellow, with eyes sunk in his head and staring like a maniac, came up to me and asked if I wanted to tent with him, as his mate had died that morning and he would share his place with me. I cheerfully accepted his offer, and when we reached his tent, which was in Sgt. D.C. Thompkins' squad, it almost made me laugh, for it consisted of a piece of an old undershirt stretched on two poles. It was full of holes, and not large enough to shelter a dog. As I looked it over he noticed my incredulous look and remarked: "Pard, this tent is good in comparison with some in here." Our rations consisted of one pint of corn-meal and ground cob, and this had to last us twenty-four hours. We did not fatten much on this, you may be sure. When I was taken prisoner I weighed 165 pounds, and when I came out I weighed ninety-six pounds, and I was considered stout compared with some I saw there.

HENRY DEVILLIZ

I well remember one poor fellow who was wasted to a mere skeleton by a long and painful disease, when at last he was unable to longer move around, he retired to his burrow in the ground, and without hat, coat or vest lay down there, and in his miserable louse-infested kennel resigned himself to die. Being unable to partake of one morsel of the course and unwholesome food dealt out to the prisoners, he welcomed death as the means of ending forever his miserable existence. But death was slow to answer the summons. And thus he lay day after day in a semi-comatose condition, too weak to move either hand or foot, while the lice, flies and musquitoes could be seen crawling from his nostrils, his ears and his mouth. Each morning for many days his comrades would go to his burrow expecting to find that death had closed the scene; but on their near approach, his stertorous breathing would announce to them that life was still there. It was not till after the vermin had actually eaten into his flesh, creating great sores where innumerable maggots found a burrow, did his spirit take its flight.

PRIVATE SAMUEL MELVIN

Part Eight
"If the Devil will get me out of this I will worship him."

Diary of Samuel Melvin

PRIVATE SAMUEL MELVIN
Age: 20
Company K, 1st Massachusetts Heavy Artillery, Second Corps.
Captured on May 19, 1864 at Harris's Farm, Va.

Friday, June 3, 1864. Arrived at Macon in the morning. It was quite a place. After travelling until noon we arrived at our camp Winder, Andersonville, Ga., where we were driven in next to the swamp. But Asa [Rowe] & [George] Handy bought a little lot on the hill for $4.50. I was very much pleased, for it is so much healthier. The camp contains about six acres. Capt. Wirz commands. Wrote to Caroline [Melvin] for a box, as did the most of our boys. Wrote to [First Lieut., John M.] Dow also. I hope the letters will go through, but I am afraid it will be a long time ere we get an answer.
Saturday, June 4, 1864. It rained most all day & we fared rather tough. Still we managed to live through it. Drew our rations late at night, some peas. Handy bought a rubber blanket for $5, which added much to our comfort. It is sad to see them carry the dead by into the dead house, a continual train of them all the time. How I hope that I shall live through it and be permitted to enjoy the true fruition of my life, which I have put so much confidence in and placed such bright anticipations upon. Still, if I die here I am sure that we shall die in a good cause, although in a brutal way.
Sunday, June 5, 1864. Here we are in the same old pen. We fixed our habitation some and made it somewhat better. But then, O Lord! Hasten our release! Only think, if we were at the forts just one short month from today we should be honorably discharged. But how I regret, how I sigh to think of our deplorable condition. Still men have lived through rougher scenes than this, and if I take good care of myself, am very hopeful. But 'tis sad to see the dead go out, 100 per day. I have been a little ill, the beans gave me a very bad state of the stomach, but I think I shall be better tomorrow. We

look to our condition at the forts with as much joy as when there we did for a discharge, and more too.

Monday, June 6, 1864. The same as usual. Staid in our humble dwelling most of the time. It is such. It is life, and that is all. My stomach felt very much better, and I am very thankful indeed. Asa Rowe is in a bad state, and we are all in a deplorable condition, still I guess that by being prudent we will all get through it. There are millions of reports in camp relative to parole & exchange. I have come to the conclusion that we will be exchanged when the summer campaign is over, which I hope and trust will be in about three months after my time is out.

Tuesday, June 7, 1864. Awful hot in the A.M. but we had a very cool shower in the P.M., which would have been very desirable had we had a good shelter. We managed to get a pint of rice for my 40 cts. and it went first rate and made me feel better. We are having good reports from our Army but can't believe any of them. There seem to be no signs for an exchange at all until the summer campaign is over, and I hope that it will end with the downfall of Richmond. My stomach has got regulated once more & I feel encouraged. My whole thoughts are on the joy we will have when we get in sight of our starry banner. O how I would like to see it once more!

Wednesday, June 8, 1864. Stopped as usual in our old shanty. The day was quite oppressive, but toward night it was more salubrious. We drew raw rations and no wood, but by the kindness of Handy we had a little wood. Sold our rations of meat for a pint of rice, which Asa and I ate to grand advantage because it is so easily digested. I made a grand raid and got a big plate of cooked rice which did us *"roots."* While trying to make the first one we were fired upon by the quartermaster; no one hurt. A new squad of recruits came from Charleston. I am feeling first rate today and begin to feel quite encouraged. All of us are convalescent, I believe.

Thursday, June 9, 1864. The first sound of humanity reached our ears this morning in an order allowing us to go for wood if we take the oath not to escape. The prelude was, "Wishing to do all in our power to alleviate the sufferings of prisoner's life." Asa & I ate our rice and as usual it was good. We talked of getting our ration of meat turned into molasses, which we can do by giving $2 a quart for the latter. Drew cooked rations. Learned from a reliable prisoner that Butler is relieved from the exchange commission & Smith is in his place. That is good, the first bright star that we have seen since our imprisonment. Feel first rate but weak.

Friday, June 10, 1864. Things go on about the same way. Had a small bannock for breakfast. At night we got a little molasses and made some mush. It went first rate and set well. Our squad got raw rations and no wood. We sold our meat and got quite a fund. Molasses is $8 a gallon & butter $4 per pound. Little did I ever think I would pay such prices. Handy, Asa, & I entered partnership. Handy is Treasurer. My principal thoughts and hopes and fears are that my friend Dow will get killed or not be able to fulfill his promises with me.

Saturday, June 11, 1864. Had quite a rain and with our humble shelter it was no desirable thing. We got $3 worth of molasses in a quart cup and had some bread and molasses. Handy dealt it out by the spoonful, and Asa took four, so he owes us a spoonful of molasses. Now we see what makes a thing good. We think as much of a spoonful of molasses here as we would of a gallon at home, and it costs about as much. O how I would like to see some prisoners go home! It would bring such joy to us. Tongue nor pen can never describe our privations here, nor our joy when we arrive in Wash.

free from our enemies.   O how bad it seems to be kept here after our time expires!

Sunday, June 12, 1864.   With Nat's shirt made quite a good addition to our shanty, but there was need enough of it, for we had an awful night of rain.   Handy had a rough time.   It stormed all night. Had a ration of hot corn bread and we finished our molasses, 8 spoonfuls apiece for $3.   We can't stand that.   Got $1 worth of butter, 1/4 of a pound.   It went first rate, but at home we would not have looked at it.   Great rumors in camp about our parole.   O Lord, if they were only true, how joyful we would have been!   But still we know that the time must come some time.   How true, if not for hope the heart would break!

Monday, June 13, 1864.   Came on cold and rainy today.

"When the birds cannot show a dry feather,

Bring Aunt with her cans & Marm with her pans

And we'll all be unhappy together."

This is very applicable to our situation, for it rained all day, and cold it was indeed.   At night we almost froze.   I never saw such cold weather in the North.   You can see our breath as though it was frosty. Had some mush for breakfast, and bread for supper, and crouched down in our old blanket.   It is very painful.   Still in all our happiness in this and in the other world also, is comparative.   We see those around wounded & without any shelter, & compared with them we are well off.   Rumor says Gen. Winder took command here.   Rumor afloat of exchange.

Tuesday, June 14, 1864.   Another very wet day for us.   Handy had the shakes.   He bought a blanket for $5 and slept quite warm.   Got our rations very late.   Sold our ham as usual.   One of our mess "passed to the Summer Land" last night.   They are dying very fast.   Grand reports about exchange and parole.   Would to God they were true!   I do think that we will not have to stay in here long, it is not just treatment from our Gov.   Since this cold weather I feel much better.   Corn meal gives me the diarrhea again.   O how glad I shall be when I see the little starry flag again!

Wednesday, June 15, 1864.   Took off the ring S.B. gave me, put it on again.   1100 prisoners arrived.   Joe Learned and Sam Morrison from our Co.   O how sad are the reports from our regt!   53 from Co.K killed, wounded, and missing, in the battle of the 19th, when we were taken; 11 killed, and 814 out of the regt.   Gen'l Meade issued a congratulatory order to the artillery brigade on the fight of the 19th of May.   O how glad I was to learn that Dow and Page were all right up to the 2d of June. I was painfully grieved when they told me that Dow felt very badly when he learned my fate.   He came to the Co. and enquired for me of Joe.   There is a TRUE friend, & if he will go home in July and wait until I come, it will be the happiest moment of my life, and I pray to God that such may be the case.   How I hope Dow will get my letter, but I am afraid he will not.   [Lucius A.] Wilder went to stop with Learned & M.   Got the diarrhea.

Thursday, June 16, 1864.   Another large squad of Yanks came in.   Did not see any from our Regt., but learned that ours had been badly cut up while charging the enemy's works on the 3d of June.   I feel for the Regt., and very specially for the old members.   My stomach is not right yet.   Did not eat anything but rice, and had a severe day.   Rumors that 28 transports are on the way for us from Ft. Monroe to Savannah.   Felt quite encouraged, but can't quite give it credence.   Rained in the afternoon and night.   Drew some wood.   Handy had his salt and spoon stolen.   He has the shakes.

Four men of Company F, 1st Massachusetts Heavy Artillerymen who were captured near Petersburg, Va., and sent to Andersonville. Pvt. Henry A. White (top left); Pvt. Patrick F. McGrath (top right); Pvt. Stephen W. Goodrich (bottom left); and Pvt. Francis G. Chaflin (bottom right) died August 1st from diarrhea and is buried in grave # 4516.

Friday, June 17, 1864. The immortal 17th has arrived, memorable for the battle of Bunker Hill, but I live in hopes of better things, and when they come, Glory! Rained all day as it has for the past week. My diarrhea is no better, but it is not very bad, so I am not alarmed about it yet. Lived on rice. How I *do* want to see and hear from my friends....My thoughts in the day and my dreams in the night are nothing but my liberty. Ten thousand times a day do I think of my engagement to go to England. If I can't enjoy life after this, I am not sentient.

Saturday, June 18, 1864. Another stormy day. Nothing of importance going on. My diarrhea is much better. Joe L. went to the doctor. The doctor said it was a shame to keep us here so, and so it *is* truly. Pen nor tongue can never tell the agony of mind that I and some of my party endure. Here we are with no alternative but to crouch under a low blanket and think from morn till night of our deplorable condition, & from night till morn it occupies our dreaming hours. What a recreation any employment for the mind even would be, but all I can think of is, "Fly swifter round, ye wheels of time, & bring the welcome day."

Sunday, June 19, 1864. June 16th some more of the 1st Mass. came in & report that C. Berry was severely wounded. Joe & Sam are quite sick with the diarrhea, and thus things go. Handy had his salt and bag taken from him by force by the raiders. There is the greatest set of robbers in here I ever imagined could be got together in one place. Another lot of Yanks came in from the Western Army. Handy is quite ill, and we all feel very weak and bad. Still we must try to keep up good spunk. I think one month more will take us to the land of the free. Had quite a fair day, heavy shower in the P.M. Our men divided into squads of 16 [or 10?]--Much better way.

Monday, June 20, 1864. The best report yet in the N.Y. Herald that we are to be paroled between the 7th & 17th of July. I place the most confidence in it of any. I felt the best of any yet,--all of us are better. Rained P.M.

Tuesday, June 21, 1864. Felt quite smart, stirred around some. The sun was very scorching. . . . I took charge of our squad. Sold 15cts. worth of rations. Apples, plums, cucumbers, etc., have been in camp for several days. One man shot because he accidentally got over the dead-line. Nat is quite sick, the rest of us are getting along well. Report says that the Negro question is settled. Small squad of Yanks came in from the Occidental Army, Gen'l [Samuel D.] Sturgis. He is the one that had command of us on the Fairfax trot. Every nap we all dream of home.

Wednesday, June 22, 1864. Strange to say we did not have any rain. The weather is very hot and oppressive. All we got to eat was a pint of unsalted, uncooked mush. O it does seem rough, inhuman, and unjust to keep us here! If they would only take us back to the place where I first saw the light, the happiest souls on earth we would be! . . .Dreamed last night that James [Melvin] was dead, & I put some confidence in it, but hope it is not so. I can't write more, for I am thinking of things far away.

Thursday, June 23, 1864. No rain today. A small squad of recruits came, a lot of H. A.[Heavy Artillerymen] Saw two of our regt's knapsacks, one of Co. K., No. 26. It looked natural enough. Some of the squads got fresh beef, but it was rough stuff. Had some soup for supper, did not like it. Sold one ration of bread and got some meal. More rumors of an exchange. Wish they were true & think some of them must be. How I would prize life if only once more set free or back at the old fort! O how good those blackberries and sugar, and nice soft bread and butter would go! How often we think of such things when once deprived of them. When we are *men* once more, we can then appreciate life. Here we are deprived of almost life itself.

Friday, June 24, 1864. Today my mind wanders back 3 years, when at 12 o'clock I left Lawrence [Massachusetts] for Fort Warren. 3 years ago today the immortal 14th went into camp. 3 years ago today I left my friends and kindred, mother and James, & more especially my L. friends. My mind still clings to the shady streets of L., and the many fine times I have had there. But now all is different, no joy nor gladness is left. Perhaps too I might refer to my soldier comrades who now lie buried in the cold ground, some even without a covering. How many, alas, have perished since 6 weeks next Sunday. Awful hot. Nothing of importance is going on, the same dull deplorable life. Diarrhea again. How good a word from friends would be!

Saturday, June 25, 1864. Very hot, no rain, rations very late. I lived on bread, could not sell my meat. Put some meal to soak for beer. Joe sold his pailful quick. Sam is in poor spirits, but I am getting as well as could be expected. But then, I am almost distracted, for things are dubious here indeed, and all we have to console us is to hope for better things. The seeming joy is great, that I have in thinking of the joy that I will have when I see the Stars & Stripes, for then I soon will see my friends. Orders came to give back the money taken from old prisoners. That is [a] good indication, but money nor anything can ever compensate us for one week's stop here.

Sunday, June 26, 1864. The best move yet. Joe Learned came up here, making it much more pleasant for us all. A very small lot of Yanks came in from Sherman's Army. The weather is very hot, & were it not for the hopes of the future our hearts would break. Got mush and meal, very good for this accursed land. The letters stopped going, for what reason we know not. No arrivals from Grant's Army for a long time, hope there will be no more from any army. Such living as we get here is heart rending. How we would like to step into the Pearl eating-house, cor. Milk St., or Marston's, Brattle St.

Monday, June 27, 1864. Saw a little of a piece entitled "The Goal of Thought," by Joseph E. Peck, in the Repository. Thought the little I saw was beautiful. Nothing of importance going on. Some 1000 Yanks came in. Some brought good news, and some bad. Rumors still fly as regards our exchange. We met with a great loss, it was our knife, & it is very inconvenient to get along cooking and cutting wood with our fingers. As for eating, we can eat with our fingers first rate now. Joe is quite ague-y. . . . I have made my mind up on going home next month, so sure that I fell quite easy, but if next month does not release us, O God, I wish I never had been born!

Tuesday, June 28, 1864. Had a good shower which made it quite comfortable for a season. A large lot of Yanks came in, about 1000. I am about discouraged. Only think, if we only had staid at the forts, only one short week from today our time would be out and that long wished for period would have come, and I should have been the happiest of men. Now I might say I am quite the reverse. Only one week more, oh how good it sounds! But now the future looks gloomy. Otherwise Dow and I would have been going home together. Now it will be otherwise, and perhaps one of us never will go home. But we will look as well as we can on the dark and gloomy picture.

Wednesday, June 29, 1864. Quite an excitement about raiders. Took 14 of them out, and the

Capt. [Wirz] says he will do what we say with them. But one thing is bad for us--we got no rations, and on as small rations as we get, it is no fun. A great squad of Yanks came in, bringing all sorts of news. I wish some of it was true. Had a good shower. Drew 4 spoonfuls of salt for 15 men; that's great! Handy and I got caught in a shower and enjoyed a stranger's hospitality. Was thinking all day, if we were only at the forts, the order would be read today for the inspection and muster tomorrow. How I looked [forward] last muster, to tomorrow's. Oh! How I doted upon it! But my hopes are vanished, & I am sad. If I were only out of this I would give all the money I ever saw.

Thursday, June 30, 1864. Not as hot as usual, cloudy, no rain. Did not get anything but a little mush and meal for 2 days. It is rough, it is bad, and to me it is almost unsupportable. How rough it is to serve our Country through so many privations for 3 long years, then, instead of going to that longed-for home of joy and happiness, be put in this pen of insatiate misery, without one consoling thought even. If anybody was ever miserable, I am since coming here. Only 5 days more, then I was expecting to enjoy life as hugely as any man could. Got out lots of raiders and tried them by court-martial.

Friday, July 1, 1864. O dear! Ain't this a tough life? July has come, & instead of bringing its anticipated joys; woes as intense have followed it. But why keep sighing? Because I can't help it.

Moved in the new stockade, and are some better situated because the pen is a little larger. From 49 to 98 detachments moved. I made some mush for supper, put the meal in before the water boiled & it raised fits with me. Had some fresh made for tomorrow's breakfast. Bought a spoonful of w. sugar for 25cts. Lost the comb that belonged to John. Was very sorry indeed.

Saturday, July 2, 1864. Here we are at this date still living on corn meal and water. Handy had a chill again. . . .H., L., & I have got a bad diarrhea again, making us feel quite blue. Made a broth out of a bone, & had some fresh meat, but I, nor any one else, could live on the rations, & in this pen. More rumors of an exchange. O dear, were they only true! I am thinking of the time I would be now having on my way home, were I in the forts where I expected to be. How true--we know not what an hour may bring forth! But one thing, this can't always last, and when it ends I'll make it up.

Sunday, July 3, 1864. Only think, tomorrow is the immortal 4th. If I were only in Boston my joy would be unspeakable. I can't imagine the joy if Dow and I were there, free and accepted, in all things as well as Masonry. There is no difference here, one day from another, and I played a game of cards, not thinking it was the day it is. My bowels are bad yet. The guard killed a crazy man for getting over the dead-line. Had two roll-calls and no rations at all. My stars, what a fuss there would have been at the forts, if we had gone day after day with no rations! But here we stand anything. What shall I write tomorrow, and the 5th?

Monday, July 4, 1864. This has been a curious 4th to me, and it has to us all, I guess. Not a sign of any celebration, but no rations. They took the detachments off and changed ours to the 51st. More rumors of an exchange. Would to God they were true! Had a smart shower, got all wet. Got a cold in the night and had a touch of ague. This is my 4th Fourth of July in the Army. 3 years ago today I was on guard for the first time in the tent at Fort Albany. I came out of the G.H. [Guardhouse] for seeing Dow 2 yrs (ago) today. I was with Dow at Albany, went off berrying with him. Thus time has passed with me. O dear, I am discouraged!

Tuesday, July 5, 1864. O for the Promethean eloquence of Demosthenes or Cicero! Today is the day longed for by me so ardently for the two long years that's past, and indeed it would have been to me a second Advent. But now it brings us no consolation or joy, for it does not send us to our friends at home. How long must we stay here? None but the functionaries at Washington can tell. But why be forever sorrowing because I cannot find joy? My faith in rumors is played out, for they say that Richmond is taken. I felt very badly with headache and diarrhea, but I think I am better. Rowe is very sick with it. I went to see the doctor, but there was none. Fixed the tent, so it goes very well.

Wednesday, July 6, 1864. Here I am a citizen, & a sad position it is for me; but I must cheer up or the despondency will bring disease. Joe went after the rations & was taken very sick, but got better before the night. This is the roughest pen that ever civilized man was put in. Here all is bestial, just like a hog pen, & hogs we must be, for like hogs we live, like hogs we act. Once in a while a good soul shines like a beacon-light ahead. Would not I like to be on my way home now with Dow? I guess yes. It would be the most intense joy I can think of or imagine. But I will be with him soon, I hope.

Thursday, July 7, 1864. Today is the day for us to start for home, & it was as I feared, no go. Can't place one bit of confidence in rumors & never shall again while in here. I have now made up my mind to stop until Richmond is captured, & then I think something will be done for us. I have got a very bad cold and a touch of the dumb ague, making this prison life not very pleasant. I dreamed last night of being paroled and seeing Dow, and the disappointment when I awoke & found myself still in Hell! I have given up all hopes of hearing from home, likewise of their hearing from me. But while there is life there is hope, and that consoles me.

Friday, July 8, 1864. One year ago we were in first rate quarters in the tents at Albany, and we had as good living as we cared about. The blackberries and sugar never gave out, and we used to eat about a quart apiece. Morning, night, & at dinner we had a good meal from the cook-house. Three times a week we had a plum-duff. My tent had a nice cool cellar, & we had a large stone jar which we kept full of good butter. Then we had a pint of milk morning and evening in our coffee, making it like home, it seems now. H. had a shake, got over it well. I was quite sick with the cold I have. A few prisoners came, no signs of any going out. I think now of staying until cool weather.

Saturday, July 9, 1864. Sad, sad news from our Co. & Regt. A lot of prisoners came in, & with them that good man, Mr. M. Emery of Co. F. He is not well. I am glad and sorry to see him. He is the most congenial friend I have here yet. I learn that Page is slightly wounded, but all right and safe. Bro. Dow slightly [wounded] in the foot. Dow still keeps in the field. I wish he would go home! Some of Co. are on the way here. McKay is Ord. of our Co., & there are but 12 or 15 for duty. Corp. Collins is dead, and one of the Hunters, & O, I sadly deplore the surviving one's fate! I will not write much until our boys come in. 30 of F. were captured. After hearing of the Co.'s fate I don't know but I am in luck. I am glad to hear that Page is safe, & I think Dow will now be out of danger.

Sunday, July 10, 1864. Today, sad news indeed I must record. I learn by Bridges that Bro. Asa [Melvin] was shot through the heart while charging the breastworks at Petersburg, on June 16, 1864. Bridges got to him just in season to stop some officers robbing his pockets. Bridges took his pocket-book containing $14.62 & a few stamps, and his Bible, and gave them to the Chaplain. That is consoling. Corp. Wm. Hills died with the diarrhea. He was a good boy, and a friend to me. It is sad, but I still have faith in my belief, & find relief therein. . . . I am mighty glad to learn that Dow has gone home & knows where I am.

Monday, July 11, 1864. Today I saw six victims hung for murdering their fellow-prisoners. They are the first ones I ever saw hung. They call them raiders. One rope broke. Mr. Emery stayed here in the daytime, & picked up where he could at night. Fry, the two Sheehans, Wiggin, Bridges, Voigt & Jackson from our regt. came in yesterday. More rumors of an exchange on the 16th inst. O if it were true! A man said he saw it in the Wash. Chronicle. How I want to go home and see my folks while I still have some to see! Now Asa is gone, if James has not survived, I am left alone. But I think James lives if he had a care.

Tuesday, July 12, 1864. One day more has passed, thank God, and it must bring us nearer the Welcome Day. More of our reg't. came in; lots from Co. F. Emery got in with a stranger. I am very glad of it. Well, if things go right, & I don't fear much but they will, I shall consider myself very lucky. To have things go right, I shall get out of here this, or early next month, find Dow all right waiting for me, & then, after settling the things at home, I will start on our life's journey. How I long for liberty! How sick I am of corn meal! O! how good it would seem even now to go to some good swill-pail and fill ourselves! I wait in hopes.

Wednesday, July 13, 1864. One more day has gone & brings us no relief. Still, if we live, *Time* must bring the welcome day. It will bring us out of the miry pit & set our feet upon a rock, & then what happy mortals we will be! But we are waiting, patiently waiting, waiting for the prison gates to be opened & for Abraham to say, "Come." Then will we bless our stars and return to our beloved friends at home. What a glorious meeting it will be! How I would like to meet Dow in the Astor House or in Boston! God grant that things will work for our good & that we may be permitted to spend the life of pleasure and enjoyment together that we have doted on so much!

Thursday, July 14, 1864. Not so hot as usual, but things go bad. As for exchange or parole, I am about played out hoping for such a thing. The Sergt's went to see the Capt. [Wirz], and he told them he would shell us till not a man was left if any attempt was made to break out. O dear, has Dow patience to wait for me? If I have patience to wait in this pen, I think he ought to have. But I am waiting, waiting, waiting, with patience. Emery is better. I am glad of it. I am not very sick, nor very well yet. I have continually had the diarrhea, & for the last few weeks I have had a bad cold, making me not very chipper. O God! Deliver us from this prison!

Friday, July 15, 1864. Saw a petition they are getting up to send to our Gov. I hope that they will send it, for it cannot do harm, & if it will do good, for the sake of humanity send it along. I am not very well and never shall be while they keep me in here. I do think that this is not fair for us to be kept here. It is unjust, for the sake of humanity, or Christianity, or anything that pretends to be civilized and much more *Enlightened*. O do not boast of your enlightened age! Away, away, while such suffering and misery are going on! This, this is shameful--it is disgraceful--& here let it rest. The weather is quite cool & all goes wrong, but Time must release us, and that is all I look for to do anything for us.

Saturday, July 16, 1864. Did not write till near night, for I felt very badly. Went to the Dr. & he did not see me, for Joe could not wait for me. I am about discouraged. O dear, I am so sick of this corn meal! The sight of it makes me sick. O how I would prize some good bread and milk! What a thrill of feeling it would send through my whole being.

Sunday, July 17, 1864. Went to the Doctor. He prescribed some diarrhea & cough medicine, but the cough medicine got spilled, so it did me no good, no good. I am in a bad condition, nothing but water passes me, & no appetite for anything we see here at all. This corn meal is awful sickening. It is too bad, too bad, but such is the case. O God! The man that will take me out of this I will call him "Prince of Kings & Lord of Lords." He to me will be a true Redeemer, I think, in every sense of the word.

Monday, July 18, 1864. Lay on my back in the tent in the dirt all day, pretty sick. This is hard, indeed, but I don't see why we must stand it. How I wish Dow would come down to see me as he did at Albany when he heard I was sick. But I only live to see it through, I think it will be all right. The weather is quite cool today, with some rain.

Tuesday, July 19, 1864. Felt quite blue. My stomach is no better, but I got a biscuit for breakfast, and some flour gruel for breakfast and supper. It did no good, only temporarily. Mr. Emery sold my meat for 20 cts. Good news from Sherman, & I am satisfied that Kilpatrick is on a raid for us & I put a great deal of confidence.

Wednesday, July 20, 1864. I felt some better, but not quite well. The rebels are throwing up breast-works as fast as they--

Thursday, July 21, 1864. Felt some better, but nothing but water passes me yet.

Friday, July 22, 1864. Here we are, still in the same place. . . Did not eat much.

Saturday, July 23, 1864. Lay very cold. The weather looks like the melancholy days, & puts me in mind of Fall, & that it was time something was done for us. A man in Co. F. died today. Drew 4 spoonfuls of rice.

Sunday, July 24, 1864. Well, here we are, but I am feeling better and am therefore in some better spirits. It is rumored that Atlanta is taken, and I guess it is. Grant seems not to be doing much & we are still here. The weather is so cold that we come near freezing, but it makes us feel better. It gives me an appetite for a good hot breakfast. But every day brings us one day nearer our release. I do hope we will not be forgotten, for our Gov., I think, after this campaign is over, will turn an eye towards us. Joe Hayden, Co. M., is sick, Emery is worse, and thus things go, but I am sure that the best of all is to keep a stiff upper lip.

Monday, July 25, 1864. Felt better and am encouraged. Think I shall stand it, but it is rough indeed. Emery is getting worse, and Handy too. The weather is some warmer and we did not freeze at night. A fellow in Co. G. died at 8 this evening through mere discouragement. That heartsickness, only known to the young men like us, can never be imagined until it has been endured. I am afraid there is a long stop for us in here, too. I see no signs of getting out of it, & it is heart-rendering indeed, but here I am. I got my turn for water today for the first time. We have drawn rice for two days & no salt. That is tough.

Tuesday, July 26, 1864. Emery sent in an application for himself to go out shoemaking, and also for me. I do hope we shall both be successful and get where we can enjoy life a little. Another fellow in our detachment died, and thus things go. I consider as my time is out and my contract fulfilled, it is the duty of the Gov. to release me, and if they don't do something for me, I must try and do something for myself. If I can get out on parole of honor, I shall do it, & shall think it no harm. I wish I could ask Dow's opinion on it. I would abide by that.

Wednesday, July 27, 1864. Ate some fried doughnuts for breakfast, & it made me sick enough. In the afternoon I had an old visitor in the shape of a chill. How I thought of Page, for I have seen him the sickest with the shakes of any man I ever saw. This is a rough place for such things, & they are bad enough anywhere. Emery & I had a wash all over, and it did feel good and do us good. I hope we will be fortunate enough to get up to Macon. O how glorious it would seem, and how glorious it would be! . . .A man shot dead for stepping over the dead-line. I call that murder.

Thursday, July 28, 1864. I felt very well indeed, but a little weak. Nothing of importance has transpired. Joe is a little ailing, but guess nothing serious. Emery is the same. I am very sorry he does not gain. Hope he will get out to work on shoes, and do something for himself, for I do consider it his duty to. I wish I could do something outside. How quick I would go, and should do it conscientiously too, for I have fulfilled my contract with the government by serving them faithfully for three years.

Friday, July 29, 1864. Today instead of having a chill, I had a very curious disease. I was paralyzed and could not move, & in great agony for a while. I think it is very strange, . . . but it prevented a chill. I got a little salt for Emery. Neely cut my hair, & I washed all over. I traded four rations of pork for molasses and got quite a supper.

Saturday, July 30, 1864. I felt first-rate in the morning, but in the afternoon I got down flat again, and no one to get the water. Handy went after some and got down too. I traded Holt's canteen for a bucket that holds four quarts. I hope that we can manage not to suffer now, but suppose that it will be hard as ever. Good stories about parole, and I think some of them are true. I sadly regret that I did not join the F. & A. M. [Free and Accepted Masons] when I thought of it.

Sunday, July 31, 1864. I am sorry to find Emery in so bad a condition. If he does not get better soon he never will. Good news about an exchange--I am putting some confidence in it, too. I felt well in the morning, but in the afternoon I had another of those cursed shakes. How painful it must be, those can imagine that have had them. I thought of Dow, I can assure you, and Page and every friend I ever had. Can't get any medicine, & I must stand and bear it. I am in hopes of a speedy release now.

Monday, August 1, 1864. Did not feel very well in the morning, & was favored with a good shake in the afternoon. Went down and washed in the morning, & got my water. A rebel minister was preaching & said we would be paroled immediately.

Tuesday, August 2, 1864. Had another chill as usual, but it was not so hard as usual, but hard enough to make me think of my friends if I ever had any. . . . I often think of what I now call the friends of Co. K., and I now look back to those happy times of social talk &c. Our quarters were good, and food, with what we could buy, was good. The stories say we are not to stay here long, & if the Devil will get me out of this I will worship him, for I am discouraged. . . .

Pvt. Adoniram E. Vining (left) and Pvt. Israel J. Fearing (right) of Company F, 1st Massachusetts Heavy Artillery, both were prisoners at Andersonville. Pvt. Fearing died from diarrhea, on July 25, 1864, and is buried in Andersonville National Cemetery grave # 3926.

Wednesday, August 3, 1864. Did not have a chill or shake this afternoon and felt quite encouraged. I am afraid that I am ill with scurvy. Went to see the doctors, but did not [see them.] What a crowd of sick! They take them to the depot, and where they take them is a mystery. They say they take them to Hilton Head, S.C. I am glad if it is so, but I distrust such good news. Emery is very ill. I cooked him some rice, but he could not use it. He has not eaten anything to-day. I long to see my folks.

Thursday, August 4, 1864. Made some rice.

Friday, August 5, 1864. [No entry]

Saturday, August 6, 1864. [No entry]

Sunday, August 7, 1864. I have been very sick with the diarrhea again, all of a sudden. I was called up 30 times in 24 hours. Rather tough, that, but I am glad to say that I ate some corn-bread and it went very well, & I think the change was good. Have not seen Emery for a day or two. No sick went out today. Gen. W. had telegraphic orders for an exchange of us. Only think, three years ago today at 9 o'clock we left Fort Warren. Uncle John followed us to the depot, and at twelve we started. Then we (John & I) were in good spirits. Now he is gone, and I am about as badly off.

Monday, August 8, 1864. Felt bad in the morning. Bridges made me a lot of rice soup and of course ate what I had left. Had rain in the afternoon and we got pretty wet. I sold 2 rations of pork to a F. & A.M. for 20cts. Was glad to get the chance. I wish I was an honorable member of that F., but such is not the case. O how I want to get out from here! Here I lie and wallow in the dirt from morning till night. O God, if I could only get inside our lines how happy I should be! We drew wood. I gave up my mess when I was sick. Rumors of an exchange. Am afraid it long ere I see my home.

Tuesday, August 9, 1864. Had an awful shower in the afternoon and we all got very wet, and a rough night we had too, in the mud and dirt. O dear, if such is life, I wish for it no more! Emery is very badly off and will not live but a short time, I am afraid. I do wish I could do something for him, but can't. My feet and face swell some, and what in the world is going to become of us is more than I know. Did not draw my ration. Some of the stockade fell in. How are you Dow, Page, sisters, and my only brother?

Wednesday, August 10, 1864. Asa Rowe died this afternoon, and was carried out and buried with the rest of the poor prisoners. I am sorry that he must so end his life, but it was so ordered to be. . . . I heard that Emery is dead, and am sorry if such is the case. I shall go in the morning to see him, and as I am feeling better I will try to take care of him some. We have had showers every day for three days, & awful bad it is too, but such is the prisoner's life. O I heard from the W. Chronicle that we are go--

Thursday, August 11, 1864. Felt quite well for me here. Went after water in the morning and was most exhausted. Found Emery quite smart to what I expected, for I heard that he was dead. I concluded to try and take care of him. Cooked him some rice and it tasted good to him. In the afternoon a shower was coming on, & up he came and asked for shelter, which we gave him. He was in good cheer and I felt encouraged. He stayed here all the time, but did not sleep much. The weather was very hot and oppressive. I felt very well for me. O when will we get out of this? I want to see my friends.

Friday, August 12, 1864. Made some rice soup for Emery, which he ate and liked, but he seemed to be worse after it, and he lay quiet until afternoon, when he was taken worse and was pressed for breath. He ate no supper, and continued to fail. I was very sick all night, vomiting. I asked him towards morning if he felt as though he could stand it long. He said "No." I asked him if he had any word to send to his folks. He said "No," and I left him. Things go the same as ever, no parole yet, and all our comfort is in Hope. How I long, long, long to see our lines!

Saturday, August 13, 1864. Found Emery worse. Laid him on his coat and saw he was dying. He passed to the Higher Life about seven o'clock and was carried out and buried with the rest of the Union prisoners. I was very sorry to see so good a man die in here. He was a firm friend, and would do anything for me, and I look for him in the bright Summer Land. I shall go to see his folks when I get home, and tell them the story. I am better, but God send us out of this Hell!

Sunday, August 14, 1864. Things are very quiet. They say we are going out of this tomorrow. I can't see it. I made an agreement with Charles Mills, Co. C., that if we can get to the American House next month I will pay for the dinner, and if any time after, he will pay for it. How I long for that American House dinner! I will have it right straight through in style. Had some beans with no salt, rather rough. How I long for something but corn meal to eat!

Monday, August 15, 1864. Today is the day for us to be paroled, but no signs of it yet, & my faith is growing less. It does seem as though we could not stand it much longer, but I am bound to try my best to live until I can get out of this bull-pen, for I want to see my folks at home. I have set out so much joy for me that I am sorry to die here, or stay here longer. Fairman died this morning. Last evening he was quite smart. I never saw men slip off so easy as they do here. They die as easy as, as can be.

Tuesday, August 16, 1864, through Friday, August 26, 1864. [No entries.]

Saturday, August 27, 1864. This a cool, beautiful morning. As Handy is very sick and probably won't survive long, there is another good man going to die in this horrid place. He says he would like to live and go home to his family, and who would not? August has almost passed and not released us, still I am confident that next month must do something for us, I am satisfied that the officers are paroled, & lots of the privates. . . . I long to see my folks.

Sunday, August 28, 1864. [No entry]

Monday, August 29, 1864. Today at half past seven in the evening, passed George Handy to the Spirit Life. he was another one of my true friends, and always stood up for me. He, like Mr. Emery, leaves a wife and four children. He owned two blankets in the shanty. He was one of Dow's men, whose word was bond. I don't write now, for this bull pen tells its own story.

Tuesday, August 30, 1864 through Thursday, September 1, 1864. [No entries]

Friday, September 2, 1864. Today I have another sad duty to perform, and that is to record the death of Friend Jonas Learned. He was sick only since last Wednesday with the sore throat, but they say it is not diphtheria, and for the life of me I do not know what it was. He died very easy, said nothing of his friends, and was but a little out of his head during his whole sickness. I took his things, and will see them safe with his folks, in Oxford, N.Y. Perhaps I would not like to see my folks!

Saturday, September 3, 1864. Today passed another friend, (I speak as an acquaintance) Charles

H. Parrish, Co. C., died this morning at four o'clock. He is from Lynn. We fixed our tent all over and it is much better. I think we are going out this month sure, and joy to the world when we are released! How I would like to see Dow and my folks. If they get us out of this month I am good for them, but if they keep us longer, I fear for myself. Joe L. died about 12, yesterday.

Sunday, September 4, 1864. Today I did more trading than I have since I have been in the stockade. After all the morning, I sold Emery's shoes for $1, then travelled all day & at last got hold of a very cheap one [?] & got it for 65 cts; it was worth $1. Got some vinegar and a pepper & made me what I have always craved. Got our beans in the morning and I ate hearty. Nat Brindley went to the hospital with the shakes, etc.

Monday, September 5, 1864. I have not been so hungry since I have been in the bull pen. Nothing for breakfast but a paltry plate of beans, & rations very late. I was so hungry as to faint and weak. I went down to the ration team and got a handful of rice, and blistered my finger. We got a good ration of molasses, 15 spoonfuls. I ate all my rations for supper & have not a thing for breakfast tomorrow. I think this is big, not half enough to eat. When I get to London with Dow I guess we won't starve like this!

Tuesday, September 6, 1864. [No entry]

Wednesday, September 7, 1864. Today I have felt quite elated, for 16 detachments have left this bull pen, & everybody says, & I expect, they are going for an exchange. But still I can't realize, until I see the little starry banner once more. Today I met with an accident that I was awful sorry for. I never felt so bad about anything. I lost my pocket book with my gold pen in it, that I prized, for Dow, Page, & I had used it for two years, a lock of John's hair, and some pretty pictures that Dow made. I want Dow to make me a present of one when I see him, which I hope will be in two weeks.

Thursday, September 8, 1864. [No entry]

Friday, September 9, 1864. Not a great many detachments went out today, yet they are taking them just as fast as they can find cars. It does look good, and still I can't fully realize it. No, I can't, when I get to our lines. It will be such a transition from Hell to Heaven that it will take a long time to realize our situation. I have not felt very well for a day. O dear, I would not be left here for $500. Money could never tempt me; no, not at all. In one week I hope to see the Stars & Stripes.

Saturday, September 10, 1864. Things are still very lively at night; they took out lots of Yanks. How I like to hear the old cars roll, for it portends a great deal. [Edward] Holt has got a sore throat. I am afraid it may be bad. How I long for the Stars & Stripes! How I long to meet Dow!

Sunday, September 11, 1864. Things went about so-so. Holt's throat is worse. I am sorry for him. We are going to move down on the brow of the hill tomorrow; it will be much better for us. Lots of Yanks are still going out. Good! I like to see them go. How I want to see the old transports & Uncle Sam's hard-tack! I think the show is good for us to go soon. How encouraged I am to think the time is so near! If I ever get on free soil, I bet I will keep there forever!

Monday, September 12, 1864. Today I have the saddest to record. Poor E.K. Holt's throat grew worse, and he could not eat anything, and towards night he was sensible that he could not live. He died about dusk, very hard indeed, choked to death. About an hour before he died he told me, if he did not live till morning, to carry his Bible to his father & tell him that he had read it through once, the

New [Testament] twice, and the whole most through again, and give his love to his sisters and mother. Got orders to be over to the gate immediately, for an exchange. Went over double-quick, forgot all my things, and lay there till morning.

Tuesday, September 13, 1864. Lay all day in the bull pen, & at night the Serg't. got us off in the first squad. He took me & [Lucius] Wilder & Nat, went to the depot, got two days of corn & pork, & started for, I suppose, our lines. Got about 4 miles when the train ran off and we had a bad smash-up. My car was badly broken, but the Powers that Be saved me. We stopped till morn on the bank, when after much fuss, we were taken to the bull pen. In the night I was taken very sick with the diarrhea, & weakened down to nothing so that--

Wednesday, September 14, 1864. This morn I could hardly stand. Wilder carried my things for me, and by the help of a cane I got along a few rods. Got down to the depot, and could not walk. Got an ambulance and took me to the hospital. It is an awful, nasty, lousy place, and I am disgusted. My diarrhea is very bad and will soon carry me off, if it is not checked, I am afraid. It is too bad, for I should hate to have my anticipations fail now, for they are so near their termination or beginning.

Thursday, September 15, 1864. Lay on my back all day. Eat not much, can't eat much; the corn bread I hate, & the rice I can't, for it goes directly through me. I have seen no doctors yet. The steward is a good fellow. I am lying in a tent on my rubber blanket, with an old Irishman next to me. Can't make him hear anything. He is most dead with the diarrhea. The next is a Dutchman, most dead with scurvy. And then the tent and blankets are just as full of lice and fleas as ever can be. As things look now, I stand a good chance to lay my bones in old Ga., but I'd hate to as bad as one can, for I want to go home.

Samuel Melvin died on September 25, 1864. He is buried at Andersonville in grave number 9735.

PRIVATE LUCIUS A. WILDER
Company K, 1st Massachusetts Heavy Artillery.

Andersonville Prison is an old story. It is something that I seldom mention unless I am among those who can appreciate it and who know something of prison life.

When we arrived at the prison, fortunately we had a little money, twenty-five dollars, George Handy carrying the funds. He was very anxious in regard to that money, for it was well known that every prisoner would be searched and all his valuables taken from him,--money, watches, knives, anything, anything of value, even his coat. As it happened, the Confederates seemed to be much excited at the time we arrived at the stockade.   At that time the prison contained some thirty thousand men.   The keepers were very anxious to get us inside as soon as possible, so that no one of the thousand was searched, and in consequence we carried in considerable money among us.   As we entered the stockade, the old prisoners, who had been there all the way from two to eleven or twelve months, were standing in a line, in rags, some of them almost nude; some of them had not had shirts on their backs for three months,--their hides the color of leather.   I looked them over.   I saw several men sitting there, nude apparently, living skeletons.   No skeleton in a dime museum would ever compare with those men.   They were simply skin and bones.   At this time I met an old schoolmate, by the name of Henry Joy of Lawrence.   He stepped up and shook me by the hand.   Said I, "Henry, how long have you been here?"   He looked very serious.   "Nine months," he said, "in this and other prisons."   I made the remark that I did not think I would remain there long.   He said, "I thought so when I entered here, but I have about given up hope."   Two months later he died.   The prison was so crowded that we could not find a place that we could call headquarters.   We were anxious to keep together our little band of six.   I happened to see a piece of ground with three or four willow poles bent over, about six by four.   I made the remark, "Here is a place boys.   Let us quarter here."   An old prisoner stepped up.   "Just come in, boys?" he asked.   "Yes, just come in.   We are looking for a place that we can fix up for a kind of headquarters."   He said, "I'll sell you my place."   I replied, "Do you sell the land here?"   "Well," he said, "there is no rule, but all of my friends have died and I am heir of the estate"; and he smiled.   We talked it over.   We decided we would purchase.   His price was five dollars.   We made our little shelter.   We possessed one blanket.   That blanket we got possession of from a rebel officer just before we went into prison; one of the boys having a fancy haversack which he traded for it.   We took the blanket and ran it over the poles.   I possessed an extra shirt.   My friend Ned Holt, of Company K, had an extra pair of drawers.   We made a shelter enough to keep the sun off of us, and that it is the way we lived for some two months.   Then we commenced to divide up.   We could not all get under the shelter at night.   We simply lay spoon fashion, one turn, all turn.   The man that was on the outside one night would be on the inside the next night.   That is the way we lived.

After some five weeks I noticed that the men commenced to fail.   There seemed to be no disease particularly, but a sort of despondency.   A man would lie there, and would groan and look up to the sky, and think of home and the old farm.   He soon passed away.   An early one to go was George Handy.   The next to go was Asa Rowe, and the next was Ed. Holt.   Ed. Holt died from diphtheria.   We were cooking together one day.   I made the remark that my throat was sore.   He said, "So is mine," and added, "You must have taken cold."   The next day he asked, "Wilder, how is your throat?"   Said I, "It is not any worse.   I think I am getting better."   It seems that he had diphtheria, and my trouble was nothing more than a cold.   The third day I walked him round the prison to see the boys.   They spoke to him.   He was like death, and he could hardly speak.   He said he guessed he would go back and lie down.   He went back and lay down.   He looked up and said, "Wilder, I never shall live to see the sun rise."   I told him I thought he might live to see the sun rise on many an occasion.   He spoke to his friend Melvin, who did not give him much encouragement, and he strangled to death.   I went outside of the tent and I shed tears, the only tears that I shed while I was inside that prison, for it did not do for a man to get despondent.

Three members of the 1st Massachusetts Heavy Artillery who were imprisoned at Andersonville. Pvt. Charles H. Shaw (top left) of Co. E; Pvt. Thomas Osborne (top right) of Co. F; Pvt. Davis M. Richardson (bottom left) of Co. F.

FIRST-SERGEANT NATHANIEL R. GRUELLE
Company G, 15th Illinois Cavalry, Sixteenth Corps.
Age: 35.

At home tonight, in thinking over the dark days when the souls of patriots were tried, I called up recollections of Andersonville. From a small diary I find Samuel Divon, 135th Ohio, who died Oct. 1. In his dying moments he spoke of his wife. Jacob Unger, Co. L, 119th N.Y., who had dropsy very bad, and my impression now is that death came to his relief. Also I find the following for the date of Jan. 23, 1865---"This is a day long to be remembered; very nearly 200 men were recruited for the 10th Tenn. (rebel). God forbid that I should ever be guilty of such dastardly and cowardly treachery; death is preferable."

While I am on the subject I will relate a little incident. Early one morning during this recruiting period a large, double-fisted fellow, whose name has escaped my memory, a member of Battery M, 2d U.S. Art., deserted his flag and went over to the enemy. As he was leaving the hospital in charge of a Sergeant of the 55th Ga., a large crowd of the boys gathered about the entrance, swearing and heaping all kinds of uncomplimentary remarks upon this massive skulker. Among them was a brave and noble little fellow about five feet five inches high, and whose weight at that time I am quite sure did not exceed 100 pounds, Rufus S. Read by name. Just as the guard reached a point about 20 feet from the gate Read threw himself in front of the big deserter and struck him as strong a blow as his weak condition would admit. The big fellow's head was doubtless proof against blows, but as the courageous Read was armed the consciousness of a patriot doing a sacred duty, his blow was much more vigorous than it would have been under ordinary circumstances. As soon as Read struck the fellow the crowd closed in, but the Sergeant drew his revolver and would have killed Read,--in fact, made every attempt to do so,--but Read was hustled to the rear, and his life saved. A guard rushed in, carried the traitor out, and his life was also saved; for had it not been for the prompt action of the guard the big fellow would have been swinging in mid-air within five minutes.

Shortly after this occured Capt. Wirz, heading a strong guard, came in and arrested poor Read. Wirz ordered him to be put in the stocks for 24 hours, but as this meant a horrid cruel death, the surgeons interposed, and Read was placed in front of the gate of the hospital in a standing position, with orders to the guard to kill him if he attempted to sit down. Again the Doctors interposed, and secured his release and return to the hospital, after standing four hours in one position. Poor Read--so noble, so brave, so true to his country and flag--was so weak that he was carried by his comrades to his little shelter, where all the loving and tender care of his friends was showered upon him. Being possessed of a strong will and determined spirit, aided by the kind attentions of his comrades and several of the Surgeons, Read pulled through. The other fellow--what has become of him?

Sgt. Gruelle died on September 29, 1888 of yellow fever.

PRIVATE WILLIAM TYSON
115th Illinois Infantry, Fourth Corps.
Arrived in Andersonville on December 26, 1864.

On the 25th of March, 1865, I left that villainous pen and was sent to Vicksburg for exchange, and was thence transferred to St. Louis, paid off, and furloughed home. As I have not seen them published elsewhere I submit herewith the

RULES OF ANDERSONVILLE PRISON
1.   There will be two daily roll calls at the prison; one at 8 a.m. and one at 4 p.m.
2.   The prisoners are divided into detachments of one hundred men each.   Five detachments will constitute a division.
3. Each division must occupy the grounds assigned to it for encampment.   No huts or tents must be erected outside the camping grounds.
4.   Each detachment must elect a sergeant.   The five sergeants of a division will appoint one of their number to draw the rations of the whole division.
5.   The sergeants are responsible for the cleanliness of their encampment.   They will each day make a detail from among their men to police the camp throughout.   Any man refusing to do police duty will be punished by the sergeant by bucking him for the rest of the day.
6.   No rations will be issued to any division unless all the men are present at roll call.   The sergeant in charge of the detachment must report every absentee.   If he fails to do so, and the missing man makes his escape he will be put in close confinement until the missing man is recaptured.
7.   The sergeant of a detachment will report all the sick in his detachment and will carry them, after roll call, to the receiving hospital.   After examination by the sergeant in charge he will leave those who are admitted and carry the others back.   He will at the time take charge of those belonging to his division who may be discharged from the hospital.
8.   The prisoners have the privilege of writing twice a week.   No letter must be over one page in length and must contain nothing but private matters.
9.   Any prisoner has the right to ask an interview with the commandant of the prison by applying to the sergeant in charge of the gate between the hours of 10 and 11 a.m.
10.   The sergeants of detachments and divisions must report to the commandant of the prison any shortcoming of rations.
11. No prisoner must pass the dead line or talk with any guard on post or attempt to buy or sell anything to the sentinel, the sentinels having strict orders to fire at any one passing the dead line, if attempting to speak to or trade with them.
12. It is the duty of the detachment sergeant to carry any men, who should die in quarters, immediately to the receiving hospital, giving to the hospital clerk the name, rank, regiment and State of the deceased.
13.   To prevent stealing in camp the prisoners have a right to elect a chief of police, who will select as many men as he deems necessary to assist him.   He and the sergeants of the divisions have a right to punish any man who is detected stealing.   The punishment shall be shaving of one half of the head and a number of lashes, not exceeding fifty.

PRIVATE A.S. McCORMICK
86th Indiana Infantry
Captured at Chickamuaga, Ga., September 20, 1863.
Paroled on November 30, 1864.

On the morning of April 24th, 1883, there alighted from the train at Andersonville, Georgia, a party of five people, and inquired of the writer whether he was aquainted with the place. In reply, I said I boarded there when Capt. Wirz ran a hotel on a large scale. Together we went over to the place where the stockade used to be. We found that on the east side but very little is now standing. I cut out of the north gate post a piece of wood containing a minie ball, and prize it very highly. I also secured three canes that grew up in my old "house" there. Both the slough and the island are grown up with willows, sweet gum, black-jack oak, persimmon, and other kinds of timber. I found the swamp itself worse than it was during the war. Even where the cook-house stood is swampy now, and the place is grown over in underbrush. I made the circuit of the whole stockade, and some of the earthworks, where the batteries stood, seemed as fresh as if they had been built but a short time ago. I found the Providentail spring just where it broke out so unexpectedly shortly after the rain storm which washed away the stockade on the upper and lower sides. It is about twenty feet from the stockade, on the north side of the branch and west side of the prison. The people of the neighborhood told us that the water was the nicest, purest, and coolest in all that section of the country--far superior both to the well water in the village and in the cemetery. We found that the greater portion of the south side of the stockade had been planted in corn, and that four or five acres on the north side was in corn also. We examined quite a number of wells on the north side, and they looked as solid as they did nineteen years ago. I threw a stone down one of them and it seemed to be thirty to forty feet deep.

The party of which I have alluded to brought a lunch with them, consisting of spring chicken, boiled ham, boiled eggs, white bread, and butter, pickles, pie and cakes. Just think of sitting down to such a feast as this inside of the old stockade at Andersonville! Fellow survivors of Southern prison-pens, I could not keep back the tears as I ate that meal under the shade of persimmon and black-jack oaks, about one hundred feet east of the spring, and remembered how many, many thousands of brave men had starved to death on that very spot!

UNION PRISONERS OF WAR AT CAMP SUMTER, ANDERSONVILLE, GEORGIA,
NORTH-WEST VIEW OF THE STOCKADE.

PRIVATE JOHN WOOL BARTLESON
Co.I, 81st Illonois Infantry
Age 17.
Captured at Brice's Crossroads, MS., on June 10, 1864.
Arrived in Andersonville on June 19, 1864.

Andersonville prison was first occupied about February, 1864, prisoners being brought from Belle Isle. Then there were some stumps and logs and the prisoners were able to construct fairly comfortable dugouts. When I arrived, all was bare, even all the roots having been dug from the ground. Before entering, the officers above sergeants were seperated from the privates and they were sent to a prison at Macon, Georgia. In that way I was seperated from my brother, Captain James Bartleson. Before the Captain left us, he traded for, and gave to me, a good woolen blanket. I already had an old bed tick, so I was well supplied. On entering the prison gate, the old prisoners lined both sides of Main Street, calling out, "Hotel Anderson; fresh fish; this is the place--order what you want, and where are you from?"

I soon was guying the arriving prisoners. Once I found an old friend, John Reed from my old Company, whom I had known from childhood. I was glad to see him and all the time after he came we were much together. He had brought in a pair of sheers which were badly needed in the prison, and he was kept busy cutting hair. He lived to get home and I always spoke of him as my Andersonville barber.

We soon numbered 30,000 on not over 15 acres of solid ground, a small place. Many Bounty-jumpers and roughnecks were among the early prisoners. They were well organized and every night raided the newly arrived prisoners. If resisted they would take a life. Every night men would come running down the narrow walk, crying, "murder!" I thought that this was much worse than fighting. To be murdered by one of our men was too much. We had no protection. Someone knew all the roughs but was afraid to report them.

In the early part of July, 1864, our camp was enlarged by taking in seven acres on the north. Now

I was in a comparatively clean place, with breathing room, some form to the small streets and locations. Now we chose or selected our bunkies or companions.   With me were, Corporal Bently Sowers, Jacob Allbright, and Jo Diltz.   I had one blanket and bed tick, one of the boys had part of a horse blanket, we got a few sticks and made a shade and some shelter.   We lay on the ground, hard clay and sand mixed.   We lay in a row and covered with my good blanket.   For pillows I had my old shoes, pants and woolen shirt.   Through the day I wore my cotton drawers and old blouse.   The vermin were crawling everywhere on the ground.   I was chewed with it from head to foot.

We four kept together for awhile, but I found one of them would lie awake to steal my food for breakfast, and one never washed and was extremely lazy, lousy and dirty.   I had a fight with one of them, and seperated from them, so far as I could, I guarded my own ration and went alone.   In a few days, Bently Sowers had a muss with them and withdrew, so we were all going it alone.   I soon saw that two men together, sharing their fortunes, would be a better plan.   Bentley Sowers was a good, loyal, clean man, about twelve years my senior, very particular.   I had not liked him very well in the camp at home, but now his qualities appealed to me.   I told him I had a plan whereby we could double on food and have fairly plenty to eat of the kind.   He accepted my proposition.   I told him we would have to make a sacrifice to begin with.   That evening he went down and drew our rations.   I went down on Market Street and sold most of it.   I bought a blade of a dirt shovel.   The next day our policy was the same.   I sold most of our rations and bought 25 cents worth of wood.   The next day I took all our salable ration down on Market Street, crying out, "who wants to trade raw rations for a cooked ration?"   The Rebels were issuing some raw rations, as meal and rice and nothing to cook it in or wood to cook it with, and part of the camp was drawing cooked food.   I traded our rations for meal, and mixing a little sour rice or mush with the meal, sweetening it up, adding a little water, and making cakes.   They looked very tempting after being browned to a finish in my cake pan (dirt shovel).   It took little fuel, applying one or two splinters or shavings at a time.   The one ration of meal would make two rations of cakes.   I never had trouble disposing of my wares.   Bentley was as good a cook as I. We later bought a two quart coffee pot for cooking rice and added a camp kettle.   We would use it for cooking and for carrying provisions from place to place.   Bentley always said how much we could eat at a meal, putting it in two piles on a short board, telling me to take my choice.   We ate twice each day, at nine in the morning and after market hours in the evening.   We always kept two or three days food supply on hand.   Through our policy of trading, I had eaten almost double rations, although never what I hungered for.   I was getting thin, but still preserved fairly good strength.

The rebel cook house was built just outside the stockade on the west and was built over the spring branch, so we caught all the filth from the cooking, although it didn't add much to the already bitter misery of our existance.   Our meal and cornbread was from meal not sifted.   Bread was baked in large pans and without salt.   When it was baked and brought into the prison for a three-inch square ration, I have seen as many as 13 flies on a portion, I did not eat the flies, but they didn't spoil the bread.   The flies were everywhere and into everything.   Nearly every man had piles and before a man completed his cleaning, sometimes the flies would infect him, as probably he would be too weak to fight the flies away.

We had begun to suffer from that dreadful disease, scurvy.   It attacked the mouth and the legs. My mouth was affected, with gums swollen and pus oozing.   My partner, Bentley Sowers felt it was worst in his legs and he became lame.   I had felt well, but now I took disentary and became quite weak and much thinner.   I could not eat.   My chum, Bentley, became alarmed, but my strong constitution pulled me through.

About the first of September, we broke our little camp at the north of the grounds and marched to the south side, expecting to take the train the next morning,--for somewhere.   There was an accident to the railroad and that caused us to be held where we were until the last of September, when we boarded cars and were taken to Savannah, Georgia.

Bartleson was later paroled at Savannah, Ga., on November 26, 1864. He married three times, had twelve children.   In a story told by one of his decendents, John Wool Bartleson was tormented by nightmares of Andersonville for the next 45 years.   At times he had an erie feeling that he was still being watched by a rebel guard. In January 1909, Bartelson planned to return to Andersonville hoping to exorcise this demon.

I was up early Sunday morning, and looked across a quarter of a mile distance, at the prison.   How I shuddered when I recalled the suffering there during the summer of 1864 and of the many poor boys buried in the cemetery.   I put in a full day; visiting from the star fort on the south to the three forts on the north.   The lay of the land was very familiar but the stockade had been chopped off, the dead line destroyed, but marker stakes were up all the way around.   I could locate my old position, also Market street.   The large spring branch was running as full as ever.   When I crossed the branch my eyes were cast upward to where the rebel sentinel used to stand at his post atop the stockade with his gun cocked and in position to shoot if some poor boy happened to reach under the dead line for a cup of clean water.   He was not there, except in memory.

After returning home, Bartleson had no more dreams about Andersonville.   He died on April 18, 1944, at the age of 97 years, 4 months, and 2 days.   It is very likely that John Wool Bartlson was the last Andersonville prisoner to give up his ghost.

Andersonville 1994: a portion of the reconstructed stockade (top left) including the North gate; view looking north, (top right) showing Providence Spring in the foreground; graves of the raiders (bottom left) in Andersonville National Cemetery; Stockade Branch (bottom right) of Sweetwater Creek.

Bibliography

Published Sources

BOOKS

Atwater, Dorence. *List of Prisoners Who Died in 1864-65 at Andersonville Prison.* Andersonville, Ga., National Society of Andersonville, 1981.

Kellogg, Robert H., *Life and Death in Rebel Prisons.* Stebbins, Hartford, Conn., 1867.

Melvin, James C./ Alfred S. Roe. *The Melvin Memorial.* Cambridge, Ma., The Riverside Press, 1910.

Royse, Issac H. *History of the 115th Illinois Vol. Infantry.* Pub. by Author, Terre Haute, IN. 1900.

Walcott, Charles F. *History of the 21st Massachusetts Volunteers.* Boston, Ma., Houghton, Mifflen & Co. 1882.

PAMPHLETS

Weiser, George. *Nine Months in Rebel Prisons.* Philadelphia, Pa., John N. Reeve & Co. 1890.

NEWSPAPERS

The National Tribune
Feb. 15, 1883; Sept. 27, 1883; Nov. 11, 1883; Jan. 10, 1884; June 2, 1887; June 8, 1893; Sept. 15, 1904; Sept. 27, 1906; Oct. 25, 1906; March 9, 1911
The Grand Army Scout & Soldiers Mail
Sept. 27, 1883

Unpublished Sources
John Wool Bartleson Memoir
      Micheal Bub Family Papers
William F. Keys Diary
      Rutgers University, New Brunswick, N.J.

INDEX

Photo Credits